The Thomas Family
Of St. Albans, West Virginia

The Thomas Family Of St. Albans, West Virginia

❖

A Family History

Second Edition

Bob Thomas

iUniverse, Inc.

New York Lincoln Shanghai

The Thomas Family Of St. Albans, West Virginia
A Family History

iUniverse, Inc.

For information address:
iUniverse, Inc.
2021 Pine Lake Road, Suite 100
Lincoln, NE 68512
www.iuniverse.com

ISBN: 0-595-33412-1 (pbk)
ISBN: 0-595-66909-3 (cloth)

Printed in the United States of America

This book is first dedicated to my parents, Don and Reba Thomas, and to their ancestors. The opportunities that I have today are because of them.

This book is also dedicated to my wife Michelle. I'm lucky to have you.

Contents

Preface

For many years, it had been mentioned that I had "Indian blood" in my ancestry. For no particular reason, on a 2003 trip to my home state of West Virginia I stopped by the State Archives to try to verify my Native American ancestry. As I investigated that question, a few hours turned into a much larger project, and I found myself engrossed in trying to learn more about all of my various ancestors. This book, a family history of my parents and their ancestors, is the end result of this research.

The focus of this book is on my parents and their direct ancestors. My primary objective is simply to tell the family story and summarize the family genealogy as best it is known. In the first edition of this book I was able to provide a fairly detailed overview of my mother's ancestors. In this second edition, thanks to efforts of helpful researchers in Maryland and England, I've now been able to fill-in many of the blanks in the ancestry of my father. In addition, various newfound cousins have provided additional photographs and stories that help enrich the family history beyond the basic genealogy.

Though I've put substantial effort into attempting to ensure accuracy of content, it is certainly possible that there are errors.

There are many ancestors identified in this book, and it can be a challenge to keep in mind just how they all fit together. It is intended that Appendix A can be of help in this regard, by providing brief summaries of each ancestor, how they fit in the family pedigree, and what basic information is known about them. For many ancestors, Appendix A also provides additional information not found in the body of the book.

A family history is never complete. Any reader with additional information on the lines discussed in this book is welcome to email me at **bobthomas7@yahoo.com**, and appropriate additions will be incorporated into future versions of this book.

I hope that you enjoy reading this book as much as I've enjoyed putting it together!

Bob Thomas
September 2004

Acknowledgements

This book is possible because of the help and support of many people.

First, Don and Reba Thomas provided family documents, photographs, and stories that help bring some of the genealogy to life.

Becky Hinton, a great-granddaughter of Nannie Jones, provided family history information that she had documented for a school project many years ago, when many more of the Jones family principals were still alive. Her late father Earnest Jones also provided some great family stories, as well as fantastic entertainment. Richard Hart also provided information on the Jones line.

A special thanks to Tom and Sue Martin for their stories, photos, and hospitality.

Sandi Lee Craig provided additional information regarding Seth Jones and his service in the Revolutionary War.

Don's sister Jean Draper provided information and stories on the Thomas and Hill lines. David Ferguson provided a Family Tree of the Hill family that enabled a whole line of my father's ancestors to be identified, and also shared many stories and photos of the Hills.

Elizabeth Goodnight, a sister of my grandfather, was very helpful with her recollections about the Thomas family, and provided many interesting photos from the early 1900s.

Toby Hurley did research on my behalf at the Family History Library in Salt Lake City. Similarly, Bob Richards of Cornwall Family Finders did research for me in Cornwall County, England. Both Toby and Bob were extremely helpful.

Ruby Dyson and the Charles County Maryland Historical Society provided a wealth of information on the Edelen line.

The staff at the West Virginia Archives was very helpful in identifying useful materials that aided my research.

My cousin Janis Tennant provided photographs of ancestors in the Jones line. Other newfound, distant cousins also kindly provided photographs. Paul and Joann Herdman provided an old picture of James and Peter Herdman, Ralph Sayre and Ada Ruth Sayre provided a photograph of David Sayre, and David Hart and Veta Hogsett Hart provided photos of John Paul Jones and his wife Caroline Sayre Jones.

Finally, thanks to my wife Michelle for her review and inputs on earlier versions of this book.

Introduction

Some of the ancestors of my mother, Reba Martin, can be accurately traced back over 400 years, to the 1500s. On her mother's side were the first of my ancestors known to have come to America, the Sayres. Thomas Sayre came from England in the early 1630s, not long after the Pilgrims were at Plymouth Rock. Mom's other known early ancestors also came to America in the 1600s and 1700s, from England, Germany, and Switzerland.

It would have taken tremendous courage and conviction for these early ancestors to leave behind all they had known, pack a few belongings, and come to the New World. The voyage across the Atlantic in those times was hellish. Death and disease on-board were a common occurrence, and the dead were cast into the sea. Once the miserable voyage was over, the challenges they faced in settling wild territory in a new country are hard for us to imagine today.

Mom's early ancestors of the 1600s and 1700s arrived and settled in what is today the Northeastern United States, specifically New York, New Jersey, and Pennsylvania.

One of my mother's ancestors, Daniel Sayre, joined George Washington on Braddock's Expedition in 1755, long before Washington would become Father Of Our Country. Some 20 years later, at least three of my mother's ancestors served in the Revolutionary War: Seth Jones, Henry Roush, and David Sayre. Seth Jones was at the famous battle of Bunker Hill, and perhaps was among those who heard the famous cry of "Don't shoot until you see the whites of their eyes!"

Some years after the Revolutionary War, Seth Jones moved from Vermont to Meigs County, Ohio, just across the river from Mason and Jackson Counties of current-day West Virginia. Other ancestors of my mother would similarly come to the area around 1800, and were pioneers in what was then a wild, unsettled area where Native American Indians would still sometimes be encountered.

Figure 1. Key West Virginia Locations

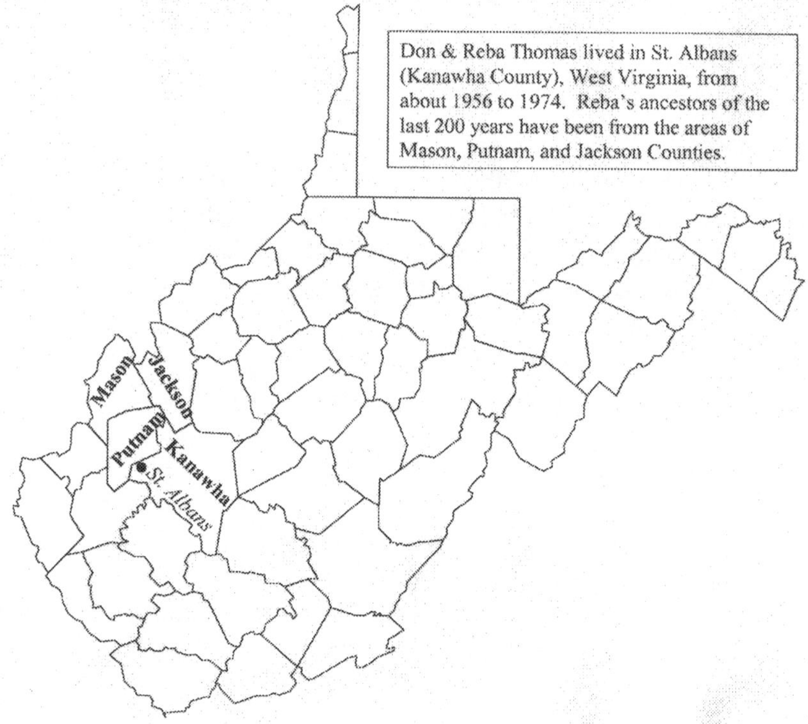

Don & Reba Thomas lived in St. Albans (Kanawha County), West Virginia, from about 1956 to 1974. Reba's ancestors of the last 200 years have been from the areas of Mason, Putnam, and Jackson Counties.

Though my Mom's ancestors on her mother's side (the Jones line) have in some cases been traced back over 400 years, ancestors on her father's side (the Martin line) have been reliably traced back only to about 1840. The Martins are thought to have originally come from Ohio to Kanawha County for salt, and when they didn't have enough money to get back home, they settled in West Virginia.

Virtually all of Reba's ancestors of the past 200 years have been farmers in the areas of Putnam, Mason, Jackson, and Kanawha counties in West Virginia. These ancestors worked hard to scratch out a living and provide for their families. Some of the families owned the land that they worked, while others were tenant farmers. If husband and wife lived a long life then they often had ten or twelve kids, but unfortunately long life was not ensured, and several of the women in my mother's ancestry died during childbirth.

Family lore is that Reba's father had a substantial amount of Indian blood. He indeed looked the part, with slender build, dark skin, sharp features, and prominent high cheekbones. However, though questions persist, to date there is no evidence of any Native Americans in our ancestry.

West Virginia was in a border region during the Civil War, and indeed the state was created in 1863 as a result of the divisions that had torn apart the Nation. One of Reba's grandfathers, James Herdman, fought for the Confederacy in the Civil War, and was at the horrific battle of Cold Harbor, where thousands of men were killed or wounded in less than an hour.

The Civil War split families, and the Herdmans were certainly an example. James fought for the South, while both his father and his father-in-law served the North. Incredibly, after the war, James and his father once again lived under the same roof.

My mother's mother, Opal Jones, never knew her father, who died when she was only four years old. Opal was perhaps the first of her line to come from remote Mason County, to "town life" in Nitro. Opal married Thad Martin, but shortly after my mother was born, Thad lost his job in the Great Depression and the family moved back to Mason County. Thad later worked in a WPA program conceived under President Franklin D. Roosevelt.

With the move to "Buzzard" in Mason County, my mother's early years would be spent in "the country." Her beginnings there were humble: she went to school at a one-room schoolhouse, she had no running water or electricity at home, and an outhouse served as the family bathroom.

The family moved back to Nitro by the time Reba was in junior high school. Thad then had a serious industrial accident, and as this was long before the days of "worker's compensation," this caused Thad to lose his job. Opal worked at several stores in Nitro, and Thad did various odd jobs, in order to provide for the family. When Reba graduated from Nitro High, her mother got a loan from Household Finance in order to buy her a new dress.

Opal was a hard worker her entire life, and passed along her work ethic to my mother, who also has worked almost her entire adult life.

Mom came a very long ways from her humble beginnings, and I often joke that she may be the only person who grew up in Buzzard, lived in California, and visited Hong Kong!

The ancestors of my father, Don Thomas, primarily came from England, including his mother and three of his grandparents. These three lines of my father's ancestry have been traced back into the 1700s. The ancestry of the fourth of Dad's grandparents, Mary Edelen, also leads back to England, specifically to Richard Edelen, who was born in 1635.

Richard Edelen came from London to Maryland around 1664. He went back to visit London shortly thereafter, having the terrible luck to be in London during both the horrible outbreak of The Plague in 1665, and the Great London Fire the following year. Richard then returned to Maryland, where he worked as a surveyor and a carpenter. His descendants in my line lived in Maryland for over 200 years, until my great-grandmother Mary Edelen moved to Washington D.C. in the late 1800s.

The Thomas line has is roots in Cornwall County, England, and has been traced back to the mid-1700s. Little is known about the distant Thomas ancestors until we get to the time of Anthony Thomas in the mid-1800s. Anthony and his son James were both tenant farmers, though James worked at least for a while as a miner.

James brought his family to the U.S. in 1884, and as the family traveled in steerage (3rd class) on a ship that advertised the lowest fares, they were clearly on a meager budget. For their start in the New World, the eleven members of the Thomas family brought a total of five pieces of luggage. The family arrived in New York, and then settled in Washington D.C.

James' son, also named James Thomas, was a "steam engineer," who worked on a Navy research vessel for a year, and then for many years ran the elevator and other equipment in the Washington Monument. Starting with James, men of the Thomas line have now been in engineering professions for some 120 years.

James died relatively young, leaving his widow Mary Edelen with the challenge of raising their five children. As this was in 1918, before women generally worked (and in fact, before they could even vote), she struggled mightily to support her five children. She relied on taking in boarders in order to make ends meet, and the kids worked as soon as they were able. Their oldest child was William "Tommy" Thomas, my grandfather, who was working as a draftsman at the Maryland archives as of 1920.

The ancestors of my father's mother, Marjorie Hill, were all from England. The Hill line has been traced back to the late 1700s. Little is known about the distant Hill ancestors, other than the various occupations of the men, including a cooper (barrel maker), a hatter (hat-maker), and an engine fitter (probably a mechanic on the railroad).

Dad's grandfather, David Hill, brought his family from England to New York starting in 1908. They are my only known ancestors who would have been welcomed by the Statue Of Liberty and been processed at famed Ellis Island, as all other ancestors came over prior to either of those being constructed. David Hill settled in South Dakota, and then around 1918 moved the family to Cleveland.

It was in Cleveland that the Hill's took in my grandfather Tommy Thomas as a boarder, and in 1927 Tommy would marry Marjorie Hill.

Interestingly, both Tommy and Marjorie had brushes with United States President William Howard Taft when they were children. The President once got off the Boardwalk in Washington D.C. to let young Tommy walk by, and Marjorie had attended a dinner with President Taft at the Governor's Mansion in North Dakota.

The first child of Tommy and Marjorie, born in 1928 in Cleveland, was my father Don Thomas. Soon thereafter the Great Depression swept the nation, and Tommy lost his job. The family moved several times, and Tommy scrambled at various odd jobs to try to support his family. In 1934 he was living with his mother in Washington D.C. when he heard of a 6-month job with Union Carbide in Charleston, West Virginia. Marjorie encouraged Tommy to take the family's savings, some $16, and go to Charleston and try to get the job. He went to Charleston, got the job, and parlayed the six-month project into a 28-year career at Carbide!

My father primarily grew up in St. Albans, West Virginia. He graduated from St. Albans high in 1946, just narrowly missing World War II. Dad then became the family's first college graduate when he graduated from Virginia Tech University with a chemical engineering degree in 1950.

A few years later, my mother and father met at a dance class in Charleston, and then married in 1954. My sister Susan was born in 1955, followed by myself in 1960.

The history of my ancestors in many ways mirrors the history, struggles, and successes of America. My mother and father's ancestors came from Europe and helped settle and build the country, fought in the battles that defined the nation, lost their jobs in the Great Depression, and eventually enjoyed America's prosperity in the second half of the 20th century.

Through the years, the Thomas family has reaped the benefits of the struggles and sacrifices of our ancestors. Life has indeed improved with each succeeding generation, such that the family has achieved the eternal goal of generations of Americans—to provide a better life for their children than the lives they had themselves.

Part 1: Reba and Don Thomas

DON THOMAS

My father, **Donald Thomas** was born in Cleveland, Ohio, on September 19, 1928. He was one of two children of William "Tommy" Thomas and his wife Marjorie.

After Don's birth, his family briefly lived in New York, Baltimore, and Washington D.C. before moving to West Virginia in 1934. Don grew up in St. Albans, West Virginia, at 1016 Highland Drive.

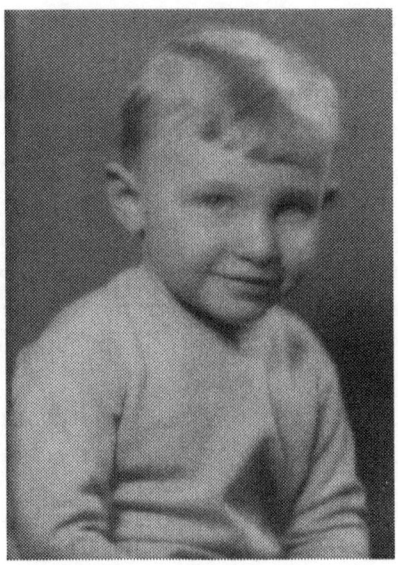

Don Thomas, 1930. Picture probably taken in Baltimore.

Don's life very nearly came to an end at a young age. When he was 6 or 7 years old, he accidentally cut his leg while doing yard-work with a sickle, and the injury resulted in blood poisoning. "I had turned blue, and they didn't expect me to live through the night," says Don. "They gave me a sulpha drug, and it ended up saving my life. I was one of the first people in the area to be treated with a sulpha drug."

Don was interested in chemistry at an early age, and his father built and supplied a well-equipped chemical laboratory in the basement of their St. Albans home. In the learning process, things would occasionally go somewhat awry. "I'd do an experiment and stink up the house, and all the silverware would turn black," laughs Don. "My parents supported me, though, and never complained."

World War II broke out in Europe when Don was ten years old, and he remembers it well. "September 1, 1939. That was the date that Dad moved the family from Charleston to St. Albans. We were driving past the Union Carbide plant, and there were newsboys out on the street, selling newspapers with big headlines: 'WAR!' and a picture of Adolf Hitler."

Some two years later, on December 7, 1941 the United States was attacked at Pearl Harbor. Don was thirteen years old. "We had just come back from church," recalls Don, "We went into the parlor and turned on the radio, and a few minutes later came an announcement of a raid on Pearl Harbor. I didn't really understand what was going on, but it shocked Mother and Dad and all the grown-ups, because they knew what it meant."

Some older kids in the neighborhood were called up for the war. "There was a fellow named Edwards that went to our church. He was older than I was, and he was going to West Virginia University to study chemistry. He was in the Army ROTC. He knew I was interested in chemistry, so he gave me an introductory chemistry book that had his name in it. That was the last I saw of him. Just before the war, he was sent to the Philippines, where he was captured. He was a POW of the Japanese, and towards the end of the war the Japanese put him on a ship from the Philippines to Japan. The U.S. torpedoed the ship, and he either drowned, or was shot in the water by the Japanese."

Don just missed being of age to serve in WWII, with the end of the war in August 1945 coming one year before Don would have been eligible for the draft.

Don Thomas as a cadet at Virginia Tech, c1948.

Don attended Virginia Tech University, and became the family's first college graduate when he earned a chemical engineering degree in 1950.

Don met Reba Martin at a dance class in Charleston, and they married in 1954. They would have two children, myself (Bob) and my sister Susan.

Don worked as a chemical engineer with Union Carbide in Charleston for 22 years. His initial work was in the area of coal hydrogenation, which involves reacting coal with hydrogen to extract liquid fuels out of the coal. He then supervised production of an acetone plant at Institute, WV, and next worked on starting a plant for manufacture of Sevin insecticide. Don then worked in Research and Development at Carbide, developing processes for manufacture of the materials for plastics. While at Carbide, Don was awarded three patents.

By the 1970's Union Carbide was scaling back operations in West Virginia, and Don took a job with the State of West Virginia, working on pollution control and pollution investigations. He had a great time in this job, doing investigative work that would regularly take him into remote regions of the state.

The family moved to Menlo Park, California in 1974 when Don took a job with Stanford Research Institute (SRI). Then in 1976 the family moved to Chattanooga, Tennessee when Don took a job with the Tennessee Valley Authority. At TVA Don once again researched coal hydrogenation and other alternatives for generating power from coal. He retired from TVA in 1993.

Don also served in the Army reserves, from 1950–1981. Leveraging his expertise in chemical engineering, Don was in the Army Chemical Corps. He was trained as a platoon leader for chemical mortars (i.e., for mortars that could carry chemical weapons, smoke-generating materials, etc.), and was later involved with procurement of chemical materials such as jet fuels. Don's objective upon entering the Army was to make the rank of Colonel, and he successfully achieved this goal.

Don has been more active in retirement than most people are when they are working. He enjoyed his work as a chemical engineer, and having the wonderful gift of having a great passion for the work that made his living, he continues to research alternative energy sources and other topics.

REBA MARTIN

My mother, **Reba Martin** was born on April 16, 1930. She would be one of four children of Opal Jones and Thad Martin.

While my father was largely raised in cities and suburbs, Mom was born in the town of Nitro, West Virginia, and a substantial part of her childhood was spent in "the country." Shortly after she was born the family moved to "Buzzard," which referred to the area around Buzzard Creek in rural Mason County. Her grandmother Nannie Herdman Jones had a farm there, and the family rented a house nearby. Their closest neighbor was a half-mile away. The local post office was listed as Nat, but there was no town there, just a general store with a post desk.

The home Reba's family rented in Buzzard had no electricity, so they used lamps fueled by kerosene. There was no running water, so the boys bathed in the creek and the girls bathed in a galvanized iron tub in the kitchen. A rain barrel by the back porch collected rainwater, which was used for washing clothes, and an outhouse served as the bathroom.

"We were poor but we didn't know it," says Reba. "Everyone around us was poor too."

Though the family was poor, they lived on a farm, and food was never a problem. In fact, Reba enjoyed "corn-meal mush" long before it would be presented in nice restaurants as "polenta." There was no icebox, but food could be kept cool in the well.

"My grandmother Jones had a screened-in porch where she kept milk, and the cottage cheese and butter she made. My grandmother Martin had a cellar built into the side of the hill. It was always cool in there, and that's where she kept goods that she had canned. We had Jell-O in the wintertime, because in the winter it would be could enough outside for the Jell-O to set."

Humble beginnings: Reba Martin in front of the rain barrel by the back porch of the family's house in Buzzard, WV, c1935.

Reba attended a school in Buzzard called Forest Hill. "Up on a hill was a church, a graveyard, and a one-room schoolhouse," says Reba. "There was one teacher, Irene Sayre, for the whole school, grades one through eight. No electricity or running water. Mother had kept me back until my sister Edrie was old enough to go, so that I wouldn't have to walk to school alone."

Her father had a car before the Depression, but the family did not have a car when they lived at Buzzard. Reba tells a favorite family story about how she outran a car one of the first times she saw one, when she was about ten years old.

"I was coming back from Grandmas on a little one-lane road. I didn't know what to do when I saw the car, so I started running. I ran all the way home with the car behind me. My mother said 'Reba, you should know you can't outrun a car,' and I said 'well I did, didn't I!'"

"Sometimes we'd pile into the horse-drawn wagon—pulled by my Uncle Clive's horses John and Charlie—and go to Point Pleasant," says Reba. "That was great fun! Point Pleasant was the closest town, and we'd go there if we needed a doctor, or needed anything that the general store in Nat didn't have."

Later, though, the family would get a car of their own, though it wasn't a straight cash deal. "My father got a car for something like $5 or $10 and a hog!" says Reba.

When Reba was about twelve years old, her father got a job in Nitro, so the family moved back from Buzzard.

Nitro—A World War I "Powder Town"

The interesting name of "Nitro" was given to Reba's hometown as a result of its roots in explosives manufacturing in the World War I era. Nitro was largely built around "Explosives Plant C," a federally funded project that cost $80M, which was a substantial sum at the time.

The location was perhaps selected for both the availability of key natural resources in the region, as well as the relative remoteness of the area. Interestingly, the plant began operations only one week before World War I was concluded, and was then immediately shut. However, the infrastructure and people required for building the plant helped position Nitro and the Kanawha Valley for longer-term development of the chemical industry that would later employ both Don Thomas and his father.

The homes that were built in Nitro to house employees of the plant were sometimes referred to as "World War I bungalows." To this day there are still many of these "bungalows" in Nitro.[1]

"After we moved back to Nitro I went to Rock Branch School, close to where Grandma Martin lived. I think the teacher's name was Mr. McClanahan. I remember he'd whip kids with his belt. Then I went to Sattes School for a year, and then to Nitro High for grades 9–12. Edrie and I both graduated from high school in 1948. I remember how my mother got a loan from Household Finance to buy each of us a graduation outfit."

Reba has worked since she was a teenager. "The lady who taught Home Economics at Nitro High would pay two girls at a time to clean her house in the evenings. We'd do the work, and eat anything we could find in the house. Then my first real job was also during high school, at the movie theatre in Nitro. It was segregated, and black people had to sit in front on the sides. I worked there until I finished high school. Then I worked at the phone company in Nitro, where the switchboard was in a lady's house. I was a switchboard operator, connecting the lines by hand."

Reba Martin's engagement picture, 1954.

Reba took a break from working while her children were young, then went back to work when the family moved to Menlo Park, California, in 1974. "In

California, I worked as a secretary at Allstate in Menlo Park. I worked there until we moved to Tennessee, when I took a job at Sears. At Sears I worked in an office for all the buyers, and when they later closed that office, I got a job as a personnel assistant."

Reba has continued to work at various administrative and retail positions, and works today at a high-end leather goods store. She has come a very long way in life, and I often joke with Mom that she is probably the only person who grew up in Buzzard, lived in California, and visited Hong Kong!

Don and Reba had two children, myself and my sister Susan. Susie married Jim Wulf in 1976, and their son Matthew is Don and Reba's grandchild. I married Michelle Hernandez in 1992.

Don and Reba Thomas currently live in Chattanooga, Tennessee, and celebrated their 50th wedding anniversary in 2004. They have a lot to be very proud of. Don served his country in the military, and they both worked hard to support the family, support my sister and I in every way they could, and put both of us through college. They gave my sister and I the type of lives that are beyond the wildest dreams of our ancestors when they came to America many years ago.

Part 2: Ancestors of Reba Martin

Many of Reba's ancestors have been traced back through the 1800s, 1700s, and in some cases even earlier. To put into context the times and issues of the world that these ancestors knew, the following timelines show some of the key milestones in American history, and some of Reba's ancestors who lived during those times.

These timelines reflect that ancestor Thomas Sayre lived in the same era as the Pilgrims of the first Thanksgiving, and indeed he came to America not long after they did. Elijah Jones was in his fifties when the American Revolution began, and his son Seth probably couldn't have imagined that his service in the Revolution would still be remembered and appreciated some 225 years later. We can only guess what Seth may have thought of President George Washington, but since he had served in Washington's army he may have had some personal insights about the Father Of Our Country.

Silas Jones was a grown man when the first telegraph message was sent, and perhaps was in awe that this incredible advance would cut the time of cross-country communications from weeks to minutes.

I wonder if Peter Herdman always remembered where he was upon hearing the news that Lincoln had been assassinated. Peter's son James was a young man when the light bulb was invented, though in remote Jackson County we don't know when he actually saw one for the first time.

When Lorenzo and Nannie Jones were a young married couple the Wright Brothers flew in the first airplane, and by the time their daughter Opal had married Thad Martin, Lindberg had flown across the Atlantic.

Little could my mother's ancestors have imagined that someday one of their descendants would write a book about them, using something called a computer.

Figure 2. Timeline – Reba Martin Ancestors to 1800

1400's	1500-1550	1550-1600	1600-1650	1650-1700	1700-1750	1750-1800
• Columbus discovers America	• DeLeon explores Florida • Cabrillo enters California	• Drake enters San Francisco Bay • First English Colony in America	• English settlement at Jamestown • First Thanksgiving	• English capture "New York" from Dutch • Philadelphia named	• Ben Franklin publishes "Poor Richards Almanac" • Baltimore founded	• Declaration of Independence • Revolutionary War • Washington 1st President

William Sayre

Thomas Sayre

Jonas Austin

Cornelius Jones

Elijah Jones

Seth Jones

Jacob Persinger

John Rausch

Figure 3. Timeline - Reba Martin Ancestors 1800-1900

1800-1820	1820-1840	1840-1860	1860-1870	1870-1880	1880-1900
• Washington DC becomes US Capital • Jefferson 3rd President • Key writes *Star Spangled Banner*	• Monroe Doctrine • Andrew Jackson 7th President • Battle of the Alamo	• First telegraph message sent • Mexican-American War • California becomes a state	• Civil War • Lincoln assassinated • WV becomes a state • Transcontinental Railroad completed	• Grant is 18th President • Bell patents telephone • Edison invents light bulb	• Garfield assassinated • Steam turbine invented • Statue of Liberty dedicated • Combustion engine invented

Seth Jones

Silas Jones

John Paul Jones

LD Jones

Peter Herdman

James Herdman

Nannie Herdman

William Martin

Benjamin Martin

L. Wilkinson

Figure 4. Timeline - Reba Martin Ancestors 1900-1970

1900-1910	1910-1920	1920-1930	1930-1940	1940-1950	1950-1960	1960-1970
• Teddy Roosevelt is 26th President • Wright Brothers flight • Ford introduces Model T	• Titanic sinks • World War I • Panama Canal opens	• Women's Suffrage • Roaring Twenties • Lindberg's transatlantic flight • Stock Market crash	• Great Depression • FDR President	• Pearl Harbor • World War II • Atomic age	• Korean War • Cold War	• JFK assassinated • Vietnam War • Man walks on the Moon

Benjamin Martin

Nannie Herdman

Laura Wilkinson

Opal Jones & Thad Martin

Don Thomas & Reba Martin

Reba's Parents

Reba's mother, **Opal Jones**, was born in 1901 in "Buzzard," in remote Mason County, West Virginia. One of four children, her father died when she was only four years old, and she had no memory of him other than a casket in their home when the funeral was held.

As a young lady she came to Nitro to work, and found a job in a grocery store. There she met **Thad Martin.** Thad was born in 1903, and though little is known of his childhood or education, it's thought that he was educated through perhaps the 8th grade. Thad had five brothers and sisters.

Thad Martin in the only new car he ever owned, a 1927 Model T purchased for $255.

Thad and Opal married in the late 1920s, and had four children: Reba, Edrie, Eddie, and Tom.

"When I was born," says Reba. "My father was working at a garden nursery in Nitro, doing landscaping. When the depression came he lost his job, and we had to move out to Buzzard." In Buzzard, Thad helped work at the farm owned by Opal's mother, Nannie Herdman Jones.

As discussed in earlier sections, the family had no modern conveniences in Buzzard. However, a neighbor had a radio, and Thad would walk over to listen to things like prizefights and the Grand Ole Opry.

The engagement pictures of Opal Jones and Thad Martin, c 1929.

In 1935, President Roosevelt launched the Works Progress Administration (WPA) program, focused on creating jobs, primarily through labor-intensive activities. Thad participated in WPA projects to build roads and bridges around Mason and Putnam Counties.

Around 1942, Thad got a job in Nitro with Viscose, a manufacturer of rayon. He was an "Oiler" responsible for maintaining machines, and earned $26 per week. The family moved back to Nitro, and would live in several rentals.

Unfortunately, after about five years at Viscose, Thad had a serious industrial accident when someone started a heavy machine that he was working on. This was long before the days of "occupational safety" and "workers compensation," and the injuries caused by this accident caused him to lose his job.

After Thad recovered from his accident at Viscose, for many years he did various odd jobs for the Mayor of Nitro, and also earned some income by selling "night crawlers," which were large fishing worms. Opal continued to work hard, as she did her entire life.

"My mother and father ran a grocery store, two or three different times," says Reba. "We lived in the back-end of the store for a while, and there was just a curtain between our living area and the rest of the store. Then we bought the house behind the store for $3000. That was the house at 503 Dupont Avenue, where my parents lived the rest of their lives. The grocery store later became a dry cleaners, and my mother worked there as long as she lived. She was a hard worker and a good mother."

Opal and Thad making apple butter, 1950.

Thad was tall and slender, traits he passed on to his daughter Reba. "He was quiet," says Reba, "and he had a dry sense of humor." As I recall, when he said something, it was either important or funny.

I remember that he had a favorite seat by the fireplace, where during the winter he always had a coal-burning fire. He'd sit in his chair, and as a young boy I would be amazed when he'd run his hand through the flame.

Though the family was preoccupied with trying to get by, Thad did find occasional time for fishing, which was his great joy. Many of the existing pictures of Thad show him proudly holding a largemouth bass or a muskie caught from the local lakes and rivers.

Thad apparently had quite a gift for being able to grow crops, but I recall that once the vegetables were in the kitchen, he was no chef! When I was a boy I laughed at how he would take a little bit of food out of several bowls in the refrigerator, and then heat the mixture up in a single pot so that he'd only have to wash one dish.

A favorite family story from the early 1960s is about my encounter at my grandmother's house with "Great Aunt Minnie."[2] I was probably no more than five or six years old, and was supposed to visit with Minnie at Opal's house. I unfortunately thought that "Great Aunt" meant "Great Ant," and refused to get out of the car, terrified that I'd find myself face-to-face with a giant insect! To this day, I feel bad about the nice lady at Opal's house, who probably couldn't understand why one of her great-nephews was afraid to see her!

Thad Martin died in 1976, and was buried at Cunningham Cemetery in St. Albans. Opal continued to work at the cleaners, and was still on the payroll there when she died in 1981.

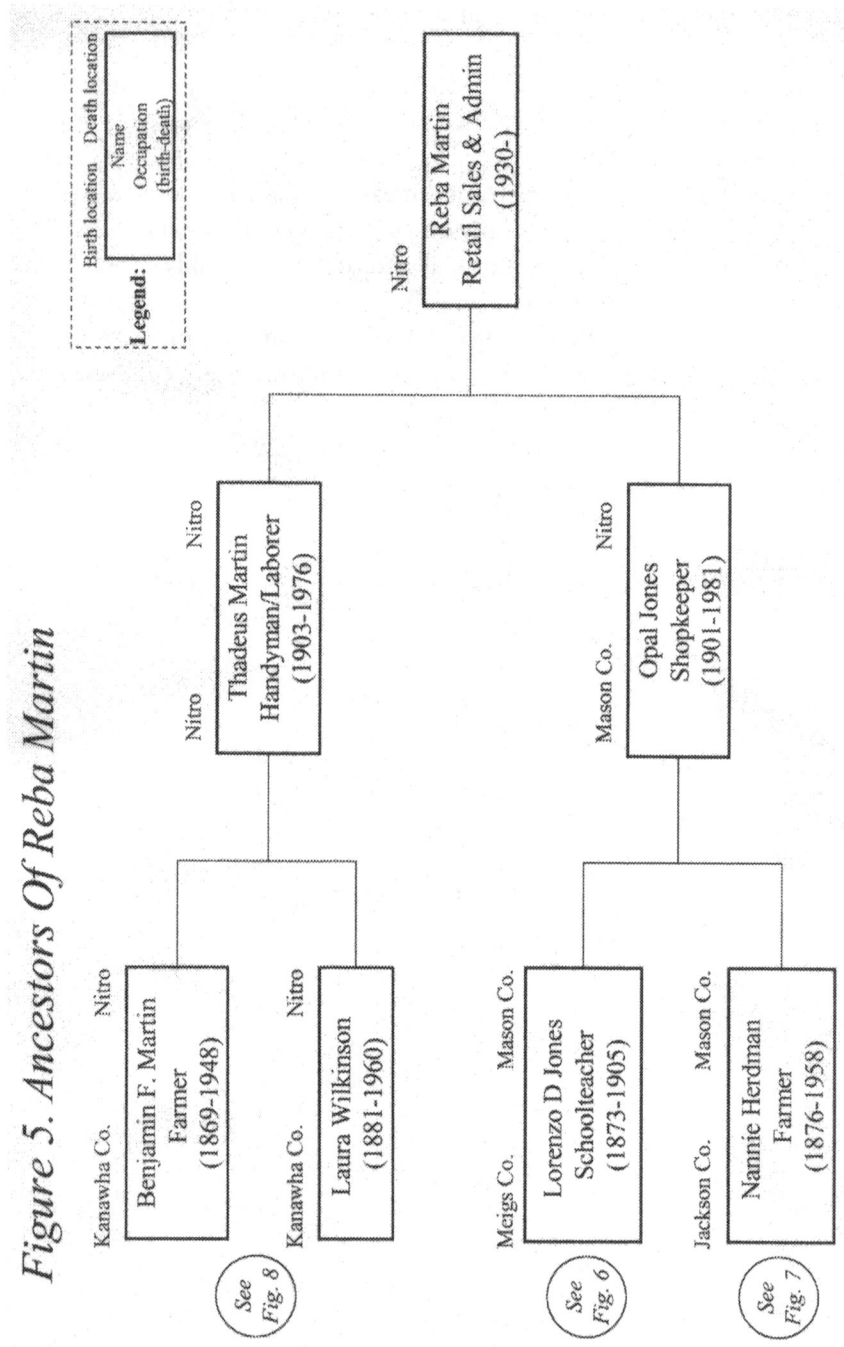

Figure 5. Ancestors Of Reba Martin

OPAL JONES' PARENTS

Opal's father, and Reba's grandfather, was **Lorenzo Jones**, who was known as "Ren." He was born in 1873 in Meigs County, Ohio, which is just across the river from Mason County. Nothing is known of his childhood, other than he had eight brothers and sisters, and they all attended a one-room school named Lone Cedar, in the general area of Creston Church.[3]

Ren attended Shelton College, on College Hill in St. Albans, and later was a schoolteacher. As an educated man, others would often come to him for help in writing letters.

Lorenzo D. Jones

In 1897 Ren married **Nannie Herdman**, and they lived in a railroad shack until they got their farmhouse built.[4] They settled in Buzzard, and had four children.

Tragically, Ren's life was cut short, as he died in 1905 at the young age of 32. It is thought that he died of tuberculosis, which was then referred to as "consumption," though it has also been suggested that he may have died of pneumonia after catching a chill while floating logs in the river.[5] He was buried at Creston Cemetery in Mason County.

Opal's mother, and Reba's grandmother, was **Nancy "Nannie" Herdman.** Nannie was three years younger than her husband Lorenzo, having been born in 1876, probably in Jackson County, West Virginia. Like her own daughter Opal, Nannie never knew one of her parents, as her mother died during childbirth when Nannie was only three years old.

Nannie's father did not think he could effectively raise a young girl, so it appears that he first had Nannie live with the family of Lewis Russell in Jackson County, and then she was sent to live with a relative in Kansas.[6] A story in the family is that she rode on Casey Jones' train on the way back.[7] In any event, Nannie came back to West Virginia when she was about 13, and later married Lorenzo Jones in 1897.

Having grown up without a mother, Nannie's life was then hit with the tragedy of the death of her husband Lorenzo in 1905, leaving her as a 31-year old widow with four children. She ran the family farm, and she ran it with no nonsense. Though she may not have been even five feet tall, she was a tough woman, and was full of energy.

Apparently like others in the area, Nannie would take in travelers who needed a meal and a place to sleep for the evening. Reba remembers a story of the visit of a hungry boy who was eating with the family. He asked for more potatoes, but was told they were all gone. "But there's some in the spoon," the hungry boy replied, referring to a speck of food in the serving spoon.

Nannie and Lorenzo had four children: Clive, Arol, Opal, and Hershel. She owned the farm, which in 1908 had an assessed value of $200, for which she was levied a tax of $2.04.[8] After Ren died Nannie never remarried, the family story goes, as "men wanted her land and wanted to boss her around, and she wanted to be her own boss."[9] Clive would live with his mother Nannie at the farm for many years.

Nannie Herdman Jones and her children (from left) Opal, Arol, Hershel, and Clive. Buzzard, WV, c1906.

Nannie had a pistol, and used it on several occasions. Her grandson Earnest Jones (son of Hershel) told stories, some hilarious, about her exploits:[10]

> *"Grandma had a .38, and she wasn't afraid to use it. Her boy Clive had a shot-gun, and he wasn't afraid to use that either. So one day some boys tried to break into her chicken coop. Grandma opened up on 'em with her .38, and Clive fired off his shotgun. Buddy, I tell you,"* [Earnest takes a dramatic pause] *"they killed a lotta chickens that day."*

"Then there was the time [in the 30's] I went over to get the cows. Buddy, I'd never seen such a mess! The cows were laying everywhere, with their eyes rolled back, and some were staggering around and making awful sounds! I thought they were dying! I ran and told grandma 'Somethin's wrong! The cows are dying and actin' strange,' and I told her what I'd seen. Grandma just shook her head and told Clive to go look up the holler. Turns out the moonshiners had put two barrels of mash up there, and the revenooers found it and dumped it into the creek. Grandma knew what was wrong. There were moonshiners everywhere in the 30's. I thought the cows were dying, but they were just drunk."

"Another one I remember is that a neighbor had two horses that kept wandering into Grandma's corn. She didn't like it, so she told the owner to keep his horses out of there. Well, he just laughed. So next time the horses came down there, she got out her .38 and shot one of them. She only shot one 'cause she knew they'd need the second horse to pull out the first one."

Nannie died in 1958 at the age of 81.

Nannie's son Clive stayed at the farm in Buzzard until the 1970s. He was a voracious reader, and the family laughed at how he even read while he milked the cows.

For years Reba's brother Tom Martin had encouraged Clive to move away from the farm in Buzzard, and to move in with him in Nitro. One day in the early 1970s, Tom visited Clive at the farm, and it was so cold in the farmhouse that a bucket of water under Clive's table had turned into a block of ice. With that, Tom brought Clive to live with him in Nitro. Clive quickly found that he liked having the modern conveniences of town, and never again went back to Buzzard.[11]

Clive Jones, in front of the farmhouse in Buzzard where he and his mother
Nannie Herdman Jones lived for many years.

Clive had mentioned that he was related to the first president of West Virginia University. The first president of WVU was Reverend Alexander Martin (from 1867 to 1875), but it is not clear how or whether he was related to the family.

Ren and Nannie had two other children. Their son Herschel ran a construction business. Their other son Arol worked as a mechanic, and was a millwright who helped construct and maintain heavy machinery at a rubber plant during World War II.

In addition to raising her own children, Nannie also largely raised three Sayre children: Dwight, Gordon, and Dorn. These were children of Lettie Jones, a sister of Lorenzo.

THAD MARTIN'S PARENTS

Thad's father, and Reba's grandfather, was **Benjamin Franklin Martin.** Benjamin was born in 1869, just four years after the end of the Civil War, in Kanawha County, West Virginia. Little is known about him. In his later years he lived in Nitro, and on his 1930 census form he indicated that he was a self-employed carpenter. He apparently helped out at Ortin Cemetery, where he was buried when he died in 1948.[12]

Thad Martin and his father at one-room schoolhouse. Kanawha County WV, c1915. The apples that kids are holding are thought to be their Christmas presents.

Benjamin Martin

Thad Martin

Thad's mother was **Larra (Laura) Wilkinson**, born in 1881 in Kanawha County. Benjamin and Laura were married in 1899, and had six children.[13] "She was a kind and soft-spoken person," says Reba. "Grandpa always liked biscuits and home-made maple syrup for breakfast, and she made it every day." She lived in Nitro until her death in 1960.[14]

Thad Martin and his mother Laura, perhaps around 1930.

In addition to Thad, Benjamin and Laura Martin had five other children: Pauline, Roy, Noble, Pearl, and Gladys. Roy died in 1958 in Nitro.[15] Noble moved to Michigan, and is buried there. Pearl was married to "Uncle Shorty," and the family laughs now at how the two once got in an argument and did not speak for years, though they still lived together as man and wife.

THE JONES LINE

The father of Lorenzo Jones, and great-grandfather of Reba, was **John Paul Jones.** He was born in 1848 in Meigs County, Ohio, and was the Jones ancestor who came to West Virginia, moving to Mason County when he married **Caroline Sayre** in 1870. He and Caroline had nine children.

John Paul Jones and his wife Caroline, c1900. Photo courtesy of David Hart and Veta Hogsett Hart.

John Paul would take in travelers, just as his daughter Nannie would many years later. Among those who would stay at his home were gypsies, who had given it their "mark" that his was a hospitable place. However, after an item was stolen during a gypsy's stay, they were not welcome thereafter.[16] Other travelers also caused complications. John Paul had a fine workhorse named Ben, but he was kicked in the stifle joint while being stabled with one of the travelers' horses, and after the injury Ben was never again able to perform as a workhorse.[17] Though an injury to a horse doesn't seem too significant in today's world, on a farm in West Virginia in 1900, a good workhorse was vital.

Caroline died in 1909, and John Paul later married his second wife Jane.

All indications are that John Paul was a fine man. It is believed that he donated the land for Creston Cemetery in Mason County, where Caroline was buried, and where John Paul was buried when he died in 1929.[18]

West Virginia's Secession From Virginia

Prior to the Civil War, current-day West Virginia had been a part of Virginia. However, many in the west did not believe that the Virginia government in Richmond was serving their interests. One key issue was that many in the west did not support, or at least did not have, slave labor. However, there were other issues as well, with a general concern that the west was not receiving a fair share of funds or support.

The problems had been around for many years, and were reflected in the lack of support for the Virginia Constitution, which passed in 1830 despite voters in the west rejecting it by a huge margin of about 8:1. When Virginia moved towards seceding from the Union in 1861, leaders of western Virginia immediately charted a course towards creation of a state aligned with the Union. As the Civil War raged, West Virginia gained statehood on June 20, 1863.

The father of John Paul Jones was **Silas Jones,** born in 1811 in Meigs County, Ohio.

A story in the family is that Silas was "farmed out" to a cabinet-maker as a child, such that he did not know his own brothers.[19] Records show that when his father died, 13-year old Silas was placed under the guardianship of James Hall, a relative of his father's widow Esther Ford Koontz.[20]

Silas did well for himself, as in the 1870 Ohio census he indicated that he owned $7000 of real estate, which was a considerable sum for that place and time. Silas married **Dorothy Roush** in 1833, and son John Paul was born in 1848, one of their seven children.

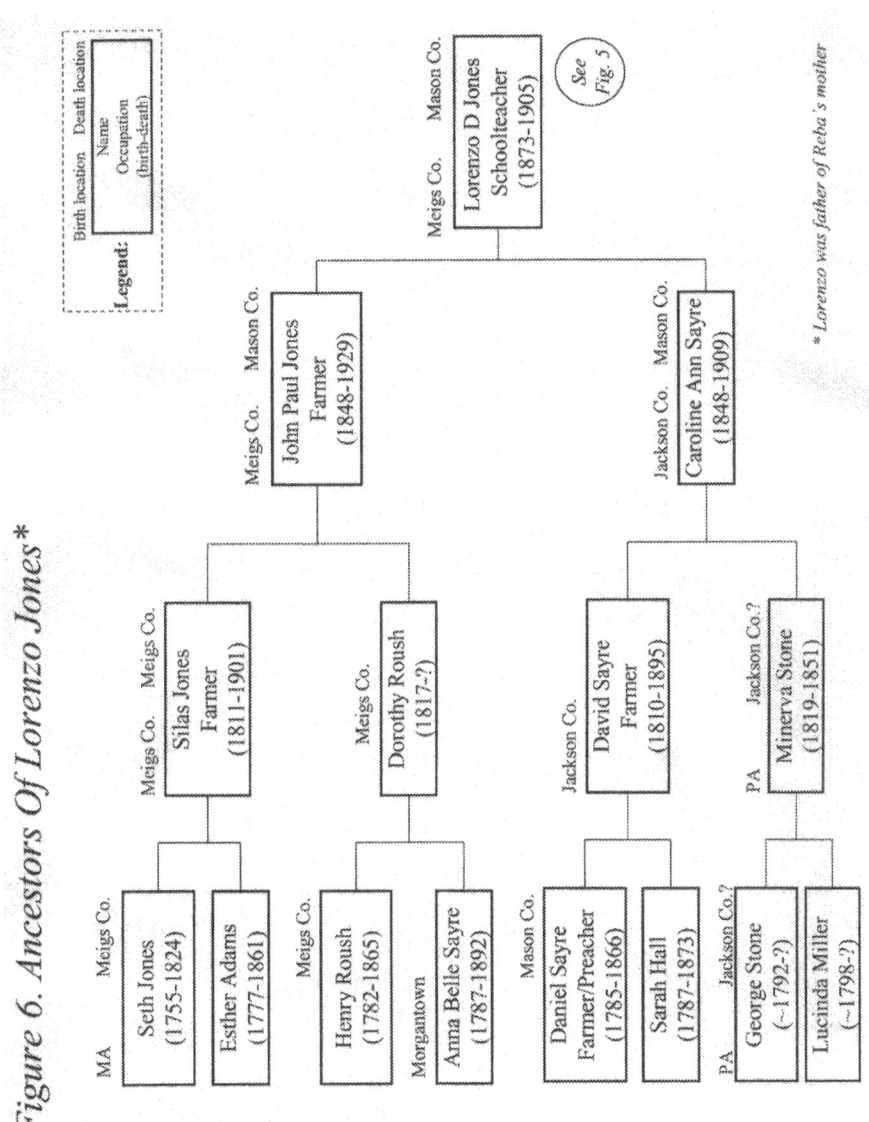

Figure 6. Ancestors Of Lorenzo Jones*

Silas was the son of **Seth Jones**, who was born in 1755 in Dighton, Massachusetts. Seth lived in Massachusetts and Vermont prior to fighting in the American Revolution. He first enlisted in Dighton, and it is thought that he did three tours of duty:[21]

- Served 8 months as a Minuteman in Colonel Timothy Walker's Massachusetts Regiment in 1775; fought at Bunker Hill.

- Served 1 month in Colonel Williams Vermont Regiment in 1777; fought at Battle of Bennington.

- Served 4 years (1778–1782) in 5th New York Regiment; fought at Battle of White Plains.[22]

It is believed that Seth and his brother Increase both served in the same Company at Bunker Hill.[23] The musket that Seth used in the Revolutionary War was a type that was relatively rare—a true 1763 manufacture from the St. Etienne Arsenal in France—and was on display at the museum at Fort Ticonderoga for many years. This weapon could be loaded and fired at a rate of six times per minute.[24] Seth told of firing his musket so much at Bunker Hill that it became too hot to hold, and he had to hold it with a strap.[25]

During the Revolution, in 1778 Seth married Sarah Pitts. Interestingly, Sarah was either the sister or niece of Peter Pitts, who had been his captain at Bunker Hill. Seth would eventually have a total of 18 children by two wives.

The Battles Of Bunker Hill and Bennington

Seth Jones fought in two of the key battles of the American Revolution: Bunker Hill, and the Battle of Bennington.

The Battle of Bunker Hill was one of the first battles of the war, fought on June 17, 1775. The colonists, a group of largely untrained soldiers, occupied and fortified Breed's Hill, just outside of Boston. The British attacked, and the 1500 colonist defenders were famously instructed not to fire "until you see the whites of their eyes." When the British approached they were turned back by a storm of musket fire. They would charge twice more, by which time the colonists were out of ammunition and had to abandon the hill. Though militarily considered a loss, the two and a half hour Battle of Bunker Hill showed that the Americans could fight the British, and provided a huge boost in confidence.

Two years later came the Battle of Bennington, on August 16, 1777. A British-led force, largely consisting of German mercenaries, was attempting to obtain food and other supplies. Their intent was to capture American storehouses at Bennington, Vermont. The Americans attacked, and a number of Canadians, Indians, and others fighting for the British quickly surrendered or fled. German reinforcements then arrived for the British, but American reinforcements also arrived in the form of a Vermont militia, and this is probably where Seth Jones entered the fray. The Vermont fighters prevailed over the German reinforcements, and the Americans had won the two-hour Battle of Bennington.

There is a story in the family that the famed Revolutionary War sailor John Paul Jones gave a gift of a sword to Seth's son Silas, and that this led to Silas in turn naming his son after the navy hero. For various reasons, this story is highly unlikely. First, Seth was a soldier, making it unlikely that he would have had the opportunity to meet and befriend the famed John Paul Jones, a navy man. Moreover, the 81 pages of material in Seth's Revolutionary War Pension File include various documents that attempt to validate his service in the war, and if Seth had been an acquaintance of John Paul Jones the sailor, it would seem likely that this would have been mentioned in the file.

Around 1800 Seth Jones moved from Vermont to Ohio, eventually settling in Meigs County, and thus was the first Jones ancestor to come to the West Virginia area. It was said that he sailed a flatboat down the Ohio River from Pittsburg, and that he then used the wood of the boat to build a cabin in Middleport, Ohio. Indians were occasionally encountered in the area, and though they generated substantial fear, there were never any problems.[26]

Sometime around 1800, Seth's wife Sarah died, and he found a slab of rock and carved tombstone for her. He was then faced with the challenge of how to raise ten kids. Help would eventually come in the form of his second wife, Esther, and they married in 1810. Silas Jones was their first child.[27]

When Seth died in 1824, his estate included land plus a yoke of oxen, a saddle, 11 hogs, a desk, and a Bible. His widow Esther disposed of Seth's estate, and apparently astute at marketing, her expenses included $3 "for whiskey on the day of the sale."[28] Esther had more than her share of tragedy, as Seth was the second of three husbands that Esther Adams Ford Jones Kountz would bury.

Much later, in 1858 Esther was granted 160 acres of "Bounty Land" for Seth's Revolutionary War service, and in 1861 she was further awarded a pension of $26 per year for his service.

Seth Jones was the son of **Elijah Jones** (1725–abt 1770?) and **Deborah Austin**. Elijah and Deborah had eight children, and appeared to have an awareness of economics by giving their children interesting names such as *Increase* (b. 1752) and *Income* (b. 1757). Elijah lived in Dighton, Massachusetts. He gave his occupation as Caulker, which likely referred to making boats and ships watertight, given that his father had a shipyard. In 1757 Elijah served as a Private in the Foot Company of Taunton. It is possible that he served in the French and Indian War, though there is no specific evidence of this.

Elijah was the son of **Cornelius Jones,** who built boats and ships for a living. Cornelius was perhaps born in the late 1600s, and lived in Massachusetts. Some 50 years before the American Revolution would begin a few miles away, Cornelius bought a shipyard in 1723 in Dighton, and also did survey work for local highways. He participated in several land transactions, selling his shipyard and other Dighton property in 1737 for the substantial sum of 500 Pounds, and then buying new property in the town of Berkley. However, it appears that the Berkley land was foreclosed in 1747 after his death.[29]

This is as far back as the Jones line has been reliably traced, though it has been suggested that Cornelius was the son of another **Cornelius Jones** and his wife **Mercy Cory**, and that Cornelius Jones Sr. was in turn was the son of an **Alexander Jones**[30].

Note that the Jones surname is of English/Welsh roots, so it is assumed that the Jones immigrant ancestor, whoever it was, came from what is today the United Kingdom, and that this person came over very early in America's history.[31]

THE AUSTIN LINE

Deborah Austin, wife of Seth Jones, had ancestors who had lived in the area around Taunton, Massachusetts, since the 1630s. The immigrant ancestor was **Jonas Austin**, who was baptized in 1598 at Staplehurst, Kent, England. Jonah came to America with his wife Constance and their children Jonah and Mary, sailing on the *Hercules of Sandwich* in 1634/35. By 1643 they had settled at Taunton, and Jonah would become a principal at the Taunton Iron Works.

The Austin line can be traced back further in England, to **Stephen Austen** (1520–1557), a laborer in Staplehurst, Kent County.

THE ROUSH LINE

The parents of Dorothy Roush (wife of Silas Jones) were **Henry Roush** and **Anna Belle Sayre**[32]. Anna Belle was born in 1782, and lived to be 105. She was one of very few people ever to live long enough to see their great-great-great-grandchild, and had over 500 descendents by the time she passed away.[33]

The father of Henry Roush was another **Henry Roush**, (1752–1831), who was one of nine brothers to serve in the Revolutionary War.[34] It is said that the Roush brothers are depicted in a painting that now hangs at the Lutheran Seminary in Gettysburg, PA. This painting shows the Rev. Peter Muhlenberg removing his clerical robes to reveal a Revolutionary War officer's uniform, and then leading the men of his congregation off to join Washington's troops.[35]

Henry came from Shenandoah County, Virginia, to Mason County (current-day West Virginia) around 1798. He stayed in Mason County for three or four years, and then moved across the river to Meigs County, Ohio, where he died in 1831.

Henry's father, **Johann "John" Rausch**, was the original emigrant ancestor of the Roush line. He came to America from Darstadt, in what was then known as Prussia, and which is now Germany. Johann was a protestant, and he may have been fleeing religious persecution.

Johann sailed from Rotterdam on the vessel *Perth-Amboy*, arriving October 19, 1736 in Philadelphia. After a few years in Pennsylvania, he moved to Shenandoah County, Virginia, probably in search of more affordable land. At this time, the Shenandoah Valley was an untamed wilderness, with herds of buffalo grazing on the land.[36]

Coming To America in the 1700s

European immigrants who came to America in the 1700s often had to endure a horrific journey by sea. Disease and death onboard were common, and the dead were cast into the sea. Young children were particularly prone to disease, and were unlikely to survive the voyage.

Food was old and heavily salted, at best resulting in poor meals and mouth rot. Water was rancid and not potable, further resulting in sickness and misery. When the ships were tossed in rough seas for what could be days on end, the passengers would cry and pray through their hysteria.

The journey to the New World took perhaps 40 days on average, but this time could vary substantially depending upon weather and wind. Once the ships arrived in America, passengers were not allowed to leave on their own unless they could pay for their passage. Those that could not were often sold as indentured servants, and would work for years in order to pay their debt. The sick fared worst, as buyers of indentured servants of course preferred those in good health. Sadly, it was common that sick passengers would manage to survive the horrific voyage, only to die in port after languishing there sick for a few weeks.[37]

THE SAYRE LINE

Lorenzo Jones mother, **Caroline Sayre**, was born February 1848, probably in Jackson County, current-day West Virginia. Interestingly, it appears that she grew up "next door" to the family of Peter Herdman, another of Reba's ancestors.

Caroline was the daughter of **David Sayre** and **Minerva Stone**. Minerva died at age 32, perhaps during childbirth. David, born in 1810, was married four times, and had his last child at the age of 57. A photograph of David is included on the cover of this book (first column, third from top. Photo courtesy Ralph Sayre and Ada Ruth Sayre).

Through Caroline Sayre, the family genealogy ties into the well-researched Sayre line, which has been traced back generation-by-generation to Bedfordshire, England, in the 1500s.[38]

The father of David Sayre was **Daniel Sayre**, born 1785, who was a farmer and Methodist preacher in Mason County. His grandfather **David Sayre** (1736–1826) served as a scout in the Revolutionary War, serving with the Essex County Militia in New Jersey. After the war, in compensation for his service he received a large grant of land in what was then Monongalia County, Virginia.[39]

By moving from New Jersey to Monongalia County, Virginia, in 1778, and then coming to the area of Meigs and Mason Counties in 1799–1800, David was the first of our Sayre line to come to the West Virginia area.

The elder David Sayre was the son of **Daniel Sayre**, who served in the French and Indian War in 1755. He served as a blacksmith in the Braddock Expedition, which was a failed British attempt to capture the French Fort Duquesne in 1755. A notable participant in the Braddock Expedition was George Washington.

Daniel's father **Samuel Sayre** had also lived in New Jersey, passing away there around 1707. Samuels father **Daniel Sayre** died in 1708, and was a whaler and a farmer in New York. He stated in his will that his children were to split the proceeds from the sale of his two slaves, and this is one of only two known mentions of slave owners among my ancestors.

Daniel's father **Thomas Sayre** was the original Sayre immigrant to come to America from England. Thomas was born in the 1590s, and was around 40 years old when he made the trip from his native Bedfordshire, England to what is now the United States, in the early 1630s. To put this into context, this would be a little more than ten years after the Pilgrims made it to Plymouth Rock.

Thomas Sayre first settled in Lynn, Massachusetts, and then sailed with a group of ten settlers to Long Island. The Dutch had previously settled the area, and just a few years before Peter Minuit had purchased Manhattan for $24 worth of trinkets. Upon reaching Long Island, the group of Thomas Sayre was arrested by the Dutch. The group was released after promising to leave the area, and then purchased land from the Indians and founded Southampton, Long Island, New York. At Southampton, whales apparently drifted ashore with some regularity, and the settlers developed processes for cleaning the whales and distributing the meat. This group of settlers built what may have been the first house built by an Englishman in New York, and this house stood until 1912.

The Will of Thomas Sayre, 1669

Thomas Sayre, a distant relative of Opal Jones, was the first of the Sayre line to come to America. The contents of his will is shown here:[40]

Thomas Sayre 1597–1670.
Southampton, NY
Vol 1 page 63
Written September 16, 1669

The last Will and testament of Thomas Sayre late of Southampton dec In ye name of God Amen.

    I Thomas Sayer of South-Hampton on Long Island in Com Nov Yorke being in perfect strength of Memory blessed be ye Lord for it, but weake of Body + not knowing ye day of my Appointed Change doe make this my last Will and Testamt in manner following.

Inpris I give + freely bequeath my Soule unto God that gave it + my Body unto Earth from whence it was first taken.

2ly I give unto my Sonne ffrancis Sayer 2 Acres of Land lyeing next unto his own in Copt Neck in ye great Playnes + 2 Acres more of Land lyeing in ye Eight Acre Lotts in ye said Great Playnes, A Pewt fflagon, a Pewter Bowl, + great Pewter Platter.

3ly I give unto my Sonne Daniell Sayer two Acres of Land lyeing next unto ye abovesaid two Acres in ye Eight Acre Lotts + three Acres more of Land lyeing in the Ten Acre Lotts and one great Pewter Platter.

4ly I give unto my Son Joseph Sayer ffourty pounds Sterling to be paid to him by my Executor Ten pounds per Annum to beginne with in five yeares next after my decease, to be paid in good Merchant Shooes or other pay that will procure Hides towards his setting up of Tanning.

5ly I give unto my Daughter Damiris Atwater ffourty Shillings.

6ly I give unto my Daughter Mary Price ffourty Shillings.

7ly I give unto my Daughter Hannah Sayer Twenty pounds to be paid at her day of Marriage or when she shall be Eighteen yeares of Age which shall first happen; And that my Executor doe keep her Cow + Calf, and their Increase for her untill she be either marryed or in some other capeable way to maintaine them.

8ly I give my Household Goods to be equally divided between my Son Job + Joseph and Hannah; And that when they be divided Hannah have her first choice of ye parts.

9ly Lastly I by this my last Will + Testament have made my Son Job Sayer my sole executor to receive all my Worldy Estate, both of Housing, Lands, Goods + Cattle + Debts due to mee from any person or persons, and to pay all Debts due from mee, and all Legacyes above specifyed.

In Wittnes whereof I have hereunto sett my Hand and Seale this 16th day of September 1669

Thomas Sayer
Signed, Sealed and Delivered in ye presence of Obadiah Rogers
John Laughton

Interestingly, Thomas Sayre was baptized in a town called Leighton Buzzard. It is not known whether this somehow played into the naming of "Buzzard" West Virginia much later, but it is at least an interesting coincidence.

Thomas Sayre was the son of **Francis Sayre** and his wife **Elizabeth**. In turn the father of Francis Sayre was **William Sayre**, who was probably born around 1500. Though William's father is unknown, the Sayre line goes all the way back into the 1300s in the area of Bedfordshire, England.

It's A Small World!

I suppose all of us are related if we go back far enough, but it was still a surprise to find that Thomas Sayre is also in the lineage of some close friends of mine. Since high school I have been close to the Shepard family of Atherton, California. Coincidentally, David Shepard has also done substantial genealogy research, and discovered that he too is an ancestor of Thomas Sayre! Though Thomas Sayre has thousands of descendents, it still was remarkable to discover that I was coincidentally a distant relative of some close friends, particularly considering that we were born on opposite end of the continent, and that we met by chance in California.

THE HERDMAN LINE

Nannie Herdman's father was **James Madison ("Polk") Herdman**, who was born in 1845 in Jackson County, current-day West Virginia.[41] He fought in the Civil War, enlisting for the Confederacy in 1862, and served in Company B of the 22nd Virginia Infantry. James was in the War for almost three years, and was apparently at the horrific battle of Cold Harbor in 1864.[42] He was wounded but survived, left the Confederate army, and signed an allegiance to the Union in February 1865.[43]

It is not known specifically why James sometimes used the name of "Polk," but his Civil War service records confirm that he indeed enrolled under this name. The U.S. President from 1845–1849 had been James Polk, a Southerner who was a protégé of Stonewall Jackson, so perhaps this appealed to young James.

James Herdman In The Civil War

James Herdman served as a Private in Company B of the 22nd Virginia Infantry. Though details of his service are generally unknown, by piecing together his service records with the history of the unit, it is possible to get a general idea about his time in the service.[44]

During the early days of the Civil War, the Kanawha Valley was of military interest as the area had salt, which was critical in order to cure meat for soldiers on the move. The Confederates, through the efforts of the 22nd and other units, scored early successes in Kanawha Valley. However, with Union troops closing in, the Confederates withdrew from the Kanawha Valley in July 1861.

In September 1862 the Confederates briefly regained control of Charleston, and this victory helped with local recruiting efforts. It was during this time that 17-year old James Herdman enrolled, on September 22, 1862, with a 3-year commitment. Like many others in the unit, he likely did not recognize that he would soon be leaving the Kanawha Valley area for the duration of the war. After a few minor skirmishes, the 22nd settled at Lewisburg for the winter, and would stay there until April 1863.

On April 13, 1863 the 22nd joined with six other units in what would become known as the Jones-Imboden raid. The aim of this raid into what is now northern West Virginia was to destroy bridges and facilities of the Baltimore and Ohio railroad, take Union prisoners, gather supplies....and overthrow the Wheeling government of what would soon become West Virginia. The raid effectively accomplished some of these lofty goals. By the time the raids were finished on May 22, the group had burned 16 bridges and destroyed substantial supplies of oil, while suffering only relatively small losses of men. However, it was by no means easy. The troops, many without shoes, marched for 24 of the roughly 36 days they were out, covering a total of some 400 miles.

The next major engagement for the 22nd was in August at White Sulphur Springs. Men of the 22nd endured repeated terrifying cavalry charges by the Union but held their ground, and the Confederate victory was to the credit of the Commanding officer of the 22nd, Colonel George Patton, who had been a lawyer in Charleston before the war. However, in November many of the same troops would clash again at Droop Mountain, and this time the Confederates were routed. In December, the 22nd went into winter quarters outside Lewisburg.

With incessant marching, poor conditions, lack of sufficient clothing and frequent combat, the year of 1863 had been trying for the men of the

22nd, and more than a few of the men decided they had enough. It was reported that on the single day of February 20, 1864, some 50 men of the 22nd Virginia had surrendered in Charleston, and wished to take the oath of allegiance to the Union.

In May 1864, the 22nd emerged from winter quarters with a roster of about 580 men, and went on the move. Interestingly, in mid-May they camped outside of Staunton, Virginia, and were visited by the young son of one of the men. This young boy, then 7 years old, was Woodrow Wilson, and some 50 years later he would become President of the United States.

By the end of May, the 22nd was soon engaged with many other units at the famous battle of Cold Harbor. James Herdman's Company B was attacked from the rear and the entire company was captured, though it appears that the Confederates soon overran that Union position and rescued the men who had just been captured.

The brunt of the battle, that James may (or may not have) missed, was horrific. On June 3, 1864, some 50,000 Union troops attacked, but the Confederates had developed excellent defenses in a short time, and cut down the attackers. "In less than an hour, thousands of Federal soldiers lay dead and dying between the lines."[45] During the 2-week campaign, casualties were 12,000 for the Union and 4000 for the victorious Confederates. This battle was the last substantial victory for General Robert E. Lee.

After a few days of rest, the 22nd was once again on the move, but the troops were tired, and nearly half of them didn't have shoes. By late June, the 22nd was losing significant strength due to desertion and exhaustion.

General Lee directed that the 22nd move into position to threaten Washington D.C., and they did so in July 1864. The objective was to put fear into the Union, and divert some of General Grant's troops from other campaigns in Virginia. The strategy worked, though the 22nd withdrew after only a day on the outskirts of Washington.

The 22nd was continually on the move during what must have been a horribly long summer of 1864. At the Battle of Winchester in September, the 22nd lost its respected commander Colonel Patton. Patton was shot in the leg while standing in the saddle of his horse, attempting to rally his men, and he would die a few days later from the wound. His grandson, General George S. Patton, would become a military legend in WWII, and would say that he took great inspiration from the courage of his grandfather in the Civil War.

James Herdman's activities during 1864 are not well understood. His service records indicate that he was absent from the November 30, 1864 muster roll due to being wounded. However, nothing is known about when he was injured, or the nature of his injuries.

The 22nd went into winter quarters in December, after what had been a disastrous year. The ranks had been dramatically impacted by combat deaths and injuries, desertion, and sickness. The 22nd was in miserable shape.

By the new year of 1865, the troops of the 22nd Virginia, and the Confederacy in general, had largely lost faith. Like many others, James Herdman decided to leave the Confederate army, and in February 1865 he took an oath of allegiance (shown below) to the Union in Charleston.

The remaining men of the 22nd saw little or no action in 1865. On April 10th, reports that General Lee had surrendered at Appomattox were confirmed, and the unit hastily disbanded.

Head-quarters, First Separate Brigade, Dept. W. Va.

PROVOST MARSHAL'S OFFICE,

Charleston, West Va., _____ 1865.

Before the subscriber, _____ Maj. & Provost Marshal, this day came _____ from Co. _____ Regiment, _____ and resident of _____ County, State of _____ and took and subscribed to the following Amnesty Oath:

"I, _____ do solemnly swear, in presence of Almighty God, that I will henceforth faithfully support, protect and defend the Constitution of the United States, and the union of the States thereunder; and that I will, in like manner, abide by and faithfully support all Acts of Congress, passed during the existing rebellion, with reference to slaves, so long and so far as not repealed, modified, or held void by Congress, or by decision of the Supreme Court; and that I will in like manner, abide by and faithfully support all proclamations of the President, made during the existing rebellion, having reference to slaves, so long and so far as not modified or declared void by decision of the Supreme Court. And I furthermore swear, that I take and subscribe to this oath, for no other purpose than that of "*restoring peace and establishing the national authority.*" So help me God."

James Herdman

SWORN TO AND SUBSCRIBED BEFORE ME, THIS 22 DAY OF _____ 1865.

Maj. and Provost Marshal.

DESCRIPTION.

AGE.	HEIGHT.	COMPLEXION.	EYES.	HAIR.	OCCUPATION.
30	5—6	Dark	Dark	Dark	Farmer

James Herdman's oath of allegiance to Union. Feb. 22. 1865

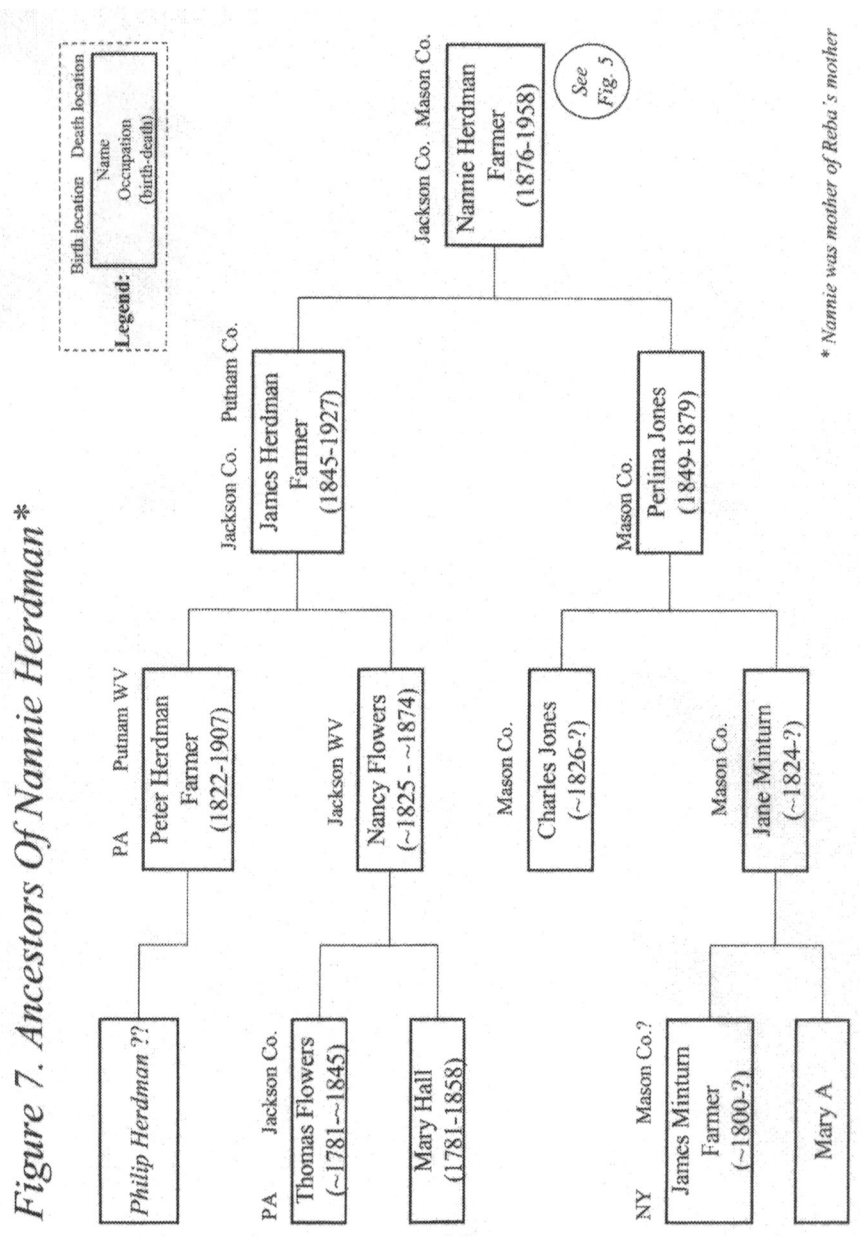

Figure 7. Ancestors Of Nannie Herdman *

There were many cases where the Civil War divided families, and the Herdmans were certainly one such family. While James fought with the Confederacy, his father served in a Union militia, and his father-in-law Jimmie Minturn served as a Union scout.[46]

The father of James was **Peter Herdman**, who was born in Pennsylvania in 1822.[47] In July 1863, at age 38, Peter joined the 141st Militia, also known as the Jackson County Home Guard. The 141st was a local Union militia, which put Peter and his son on opposite sides in the war.[48]

The 141st was not a regular army unit, and was loosely analogous to today's National Guard. Its members generally served a day or two a week, but would assemble quickly and serve as a group if needed. The 141st was responsible for helping maintain law and order, and for chasing down Confederate Guerillas. A review of the correspondence of the 141st indicates that substantial energy went into dealing with horse thieves, and dealing with lost, stolen, and recovered horses. Despite worries about the potential for substantial military engagements, none were had.[49]

The Oath of Allegiance For the 141st Militia

Peter Herdman and all other members of the 141st Militia were required to sign an oath of allegiance to the Union, and to the Wheeling government that would lead West Virginia in statehood, as excerpted below. It is interesting to note that there was a desire to ensure that members had not participated in duels:

I solemnly swear that I will support the Constitution of the United States and the laws made in pursuance thereof, as the supreme law of the land, anything in the Constitution and laws of the State of Virginia, or in the Ordinances of the Convention which assembled at Richmond on the 13th day of February, 1861, to the contrary nonwithstanding; And that I will uphold and defend the government of Virginia as vindicated and restored by the Convention which assembled in Wheeling on the 11th day of June 1861.

I solemnly swear that I have not, since the 10th of January 1860, fought in a duel, the issue of which was, or probably might have been, the death of either party; nor have I been knowingly the bearer of any challenge, or acceptance to fight a duel, actually fought; nor have I been otherwise engaged or concerned, directly or indirectly, in a duel actually fought since said time; nor will I, during my continuance in office be so engaged directly or indirectly. So help me God.

After the Civil War, James moved back in with his father Peter.[50] This must have been terribly awkward, for father and son to have fought on different sides in the War, and to then live in the same house.

During the Civil War, James Herdman (L) fought for the Confederate Army, while his father Peter (R) served with a Union militia. Photo courtesy Joann Herdman.[51]

James settled as a farmer and married **Perlina Angeline Jones** in 1872.[52] Perlina died, along with the newborn Annis, during childbirth in 1879.[53] A photograph believed to be of Perlina Jones is included on the cover of this book (upper-right hand corner. Photo courtesy Janis Tennant).

After his wife's death, James apparently had his three sons move in with his father Peter, as they are shown as living in Peter's house in the 1880 census.[54] As discussed previously, young Nannie was also sent away. James Herdman did not re-marry, and later died in 1927 at age 82.

Like many in that time and place, James could not read, and his father Peter apparently could not read or write. On his property deeds, Peter made his "mark" (an "X") and someone else would sign his name. As he was dependent upon someone else to spell his name, on various documents his surname was written as Hardman, Herdman, and Hurdman.

James Herdman's mother, and Peter's first wife, was **Nancy Flowers** (1825–1874). Peter Herdman apparently started with very little, but gradually came to own his own land. Though his holdings of $350 in real estate in 1870 were less than most of his neighbors at the time, it represented progress since 1850, when there was no indication that he had any land at all.

After Nancy died, in 1874 Peter was a mature 52 when he married 17-year old Martha McDade. Peter later died in 1907, and is buried at Cherry Grove Cemetery in Jackson County.

The parents of Peter Herdman have not been confirmed. Peter had indicated that he was born in Pennsylvania, so one candidate is a **Phillip Herdman**, who lived in Fayette County, Pennsylvania in the early 1800s and then moved to Jackson County in the 1830s. Phillip had children of the right ages to align with Peter. However, this is speculation, and it has not been confirmed that he is indeed Peter's father.[55]

Nancy Flowers was the daughter of **Thomas Flowers**, who was the first settler in Cow Run, Jackson County, in 1806.[56] There is some circumstantial evidence suggesting that Thomas Flowers was in turn the son of another **Thomas Flowers**, who served in the New Jersey line during the Revolutionary War, and who moved to Philadelphia in 1795. However, this is speculation, and no specific connection has been identified between this Thomas Flowers and the Thomas Flowers who settled in Mason County.[57]

Perlina Angeline Jones parents were **Charles Jones** and **Jane Minturn**, who had been neighbors in Mason County.[58] Jane's parents were **James "Jimmie" Minturn**, a farmer born in New York around 1800, and his wife Mary. In the 1850 census, James indicated he owned $1000 of land, which would have put him in the "middle class" of that place and time. Family lore is that James, or "Jimmie," served as a Union scout in the Civil War, which was impressive considering that he would have been in his early 60's at the time of the war.

The parents of Charles Jones are not known, though a family member has suggested that he may have been the son of a **Franklin Jones**.[59]

THE MARTIN LINE

Benjamin Martin's father was **William Martin**, a farmer born in Kanawha County around 1839.[60] All indications are that William didn't have much, as in the 1870 census he indicated that he did not own land, and listed the value of his estate as a meager $100. The same census entry indicated that he could read and write, but that his wife **Rachel Persinger** could not.[61]

William and Rachel had married in 1866, when she was 18 years old.[62] William Martin died in 1916.

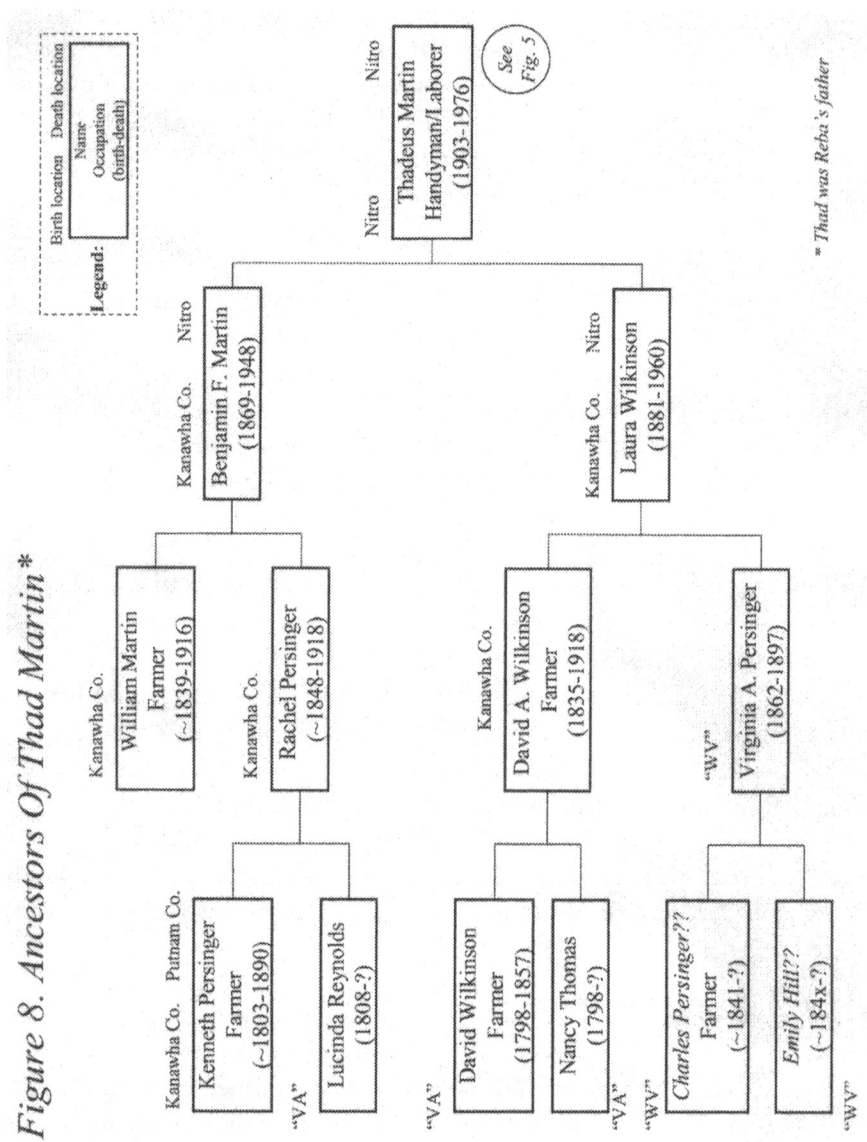

*Figure 8. Ancestors Of Thad Martin ***

William Martin believed that his father was born in Ohio, but otherwise little else is known about his ancestors.[63] Reba's brother Tom Martin recalls that he had been told that the Martins originally came to the area for salt, which was an important natural resource in Kanawha County. Specifically, it's thought that the first Martin ancestors in West Virginia came to Malden. As the story goes, the family did not have enough money to get back home, so they settled in the area.

Several possibilities have been identified for the father of William Martin. A relative has suggested that there is strong evidence that William's father was another William Martin, a Baptist Preacher born in 1804 in Virginia. However, there are several inconsistencies that leave this in question.[64]

The Hatfields And The McCoys

When many people think of West Virginia of the 1880s, what first comes to mind is the legendary feud of the Hatfields and the McCoys. By today's standards the feud was relatively close to where the Martins and many of my other West Virginia ancestors lived, being about sixty miles south of Kanawha County, on the border of West Virginia and Kentucky. However, in the 1880s sixty miles was a long way, and at best my West Virginia ancestors of the time may have been aware of the feud. For reference, below a quick synopsis of the famous feud.

The Hatfields and McCoys had a strained relationship for a number of years. This took a major turn for the worse in 1878 with a dispute over a hog, and then further degraded with a romance between Johnse Hatfield and Roseanne McCoy.

In 1882, three McCoys attacked Ellison Hatfield with fists, a knife and finally a gun, but somehow Ellison clung to life. The three McCoys were held in Pike County, Kentucky, but were turned over to a large, threatening posse led by family patriarch "Devil Anse" Hatfield. When Ellison Hatfield died from his wounds, the Hatfields killed the three McCoys, and the feud was now for blood.

The next major event would come in 1888, when a group of over twenty Hatfields surrounded the cabin of Randolph McCoy and opened fire. After it became clear that gunfire was not penetrating the thick logs of the cabin, the Hatfields set the cabin on fire. Family patriarch Randolph McCoy survived, but several of his family did not. Having now lost six of his children, Randolph was a broken man, and was done with the feud.

The following year, eight members of the Hatfield clan were sentenced to life in prison, and one was sentenced to hang. Though public hanging had long been banned, the gallows were conveniently set in a valley such that the curious were able to watch the proceedings from an adjacent hill. With the hanging of "Cotton Top" Mounts, the great feud of the Hatfields and the McCoys was largely brought to a close.

THE WILKINSON LINE

Laura Wilkinson's father, and Thad Martin's grandfather was **David Wilkinson**, born in 1835.[65] David was a farmer who owned a modest amount of land.[66]

David had 15 children by two wives. His first wife, Ann Older, was born in England around 1839. She had 4 children, but apparently died sometime after 1864.[67]

David's second wife, and mother of Laura Wilkinson, was **Virginia Persinger**.[68] Virginia was born in 1862, and was some 27 years younger than her husband. This put her in the interesting position of being six years younger than her husband's oldest son.

Virginia died in 1897, and it appears that she died during childbirth.[69] In general, it is interesting to note that in reviewing family history in the 1800s, many women had a child every 12–18 months for a very long time, and death during childbirth was not uncommon. David later died in 1918.

David Wilkinson's father, also named **David Wilkinson**, was a farmer who was born around 1798 in Virginia. His wife **Nancy Thomas** was of the same age, and together it is believed that they had 7 children.[70]

Virginia Persinger's parents are thought to have been **Charles Persinger** and **Emily Hill**, though this has not been confirmed.[71]

THE PERSINGER LINE

The parents of Rachel Persinger were **Kenneth Persinger** and **Lucinda Reynolds**. Kenneth was a farmer in Kanawha County, and neither he nor he wife could read or write.[72]

Kenneth Persinger is believed to be the son of **Jacob Persinger** and **Ursula Blake**.[73] Both Jacob and his father were born in Greenbrier County, and came to the Kanawha/Putnam County areas, perhaps in the early 1800s.

Jacob's great-grandfather, also a **Jacob Persinger**, came to the United States from Switzerland in the mid-1700s, and settled in Alleghany County, Virginia. Born in 1716, his given name was Bertschinger, and like many, he Anglicized his name when he arrived in America.[74]

Persingers And Indians

Family lore is that Rachel Persinger, wife of William Martin, was of "Cherokee blood." There is no known evidence of this, but it is also recognized that some of Indian descent did not say so on official documents, so the question may never be answered.

There certainly are though, other ties of Persingers and American Indians. Of particular note is the story of Jacob Persinger "Jr.," one of the sons of the immigrant ancestor Jacob Persinger. Though this Jacob "Jr." is not in the direct line of my Persinger ancestors (his brother Christopher was), family lore of his story is very interesting.

Born around 1735 in Virginia, as an infant Jacob was captured by Shawnee Indians along with some 30 other children, and taken by the Shawnee to the area of current-day Chillicothe, Ohio. The Shawnee raised the young boy as an Indian, until the Indians agreed in a treaty to return the captured children some 12 years later. The children were taken back to Virginia, but apparently nobody claimed young Jacob, and he made his way back to the Shawnee. The Shawnee Chief ruled that the treaty must be upheld, so the child was again taken back to Virginia. However, before he could be reunited with his mother, he ran off and again went back to the Shawnee. After his adopted Indian mother concealed him for some time, the Chief learned of the boy, and again insisted that the boy be taken back for a third time.

This time, a woman who had lost a child to the Indians many years before was brought to look at Jacob, but she doubted that she was his mother. She was only about 4'6" and he was 6'4", and the boy she lost had a scar on his ankle from a rattlesnake bite, which this boy did not have. However, the woman, (Rebecca?) Persinger took the boy in and raised him. He had only 3 months of schooling, eventually running away and settling down in a wigwam. He got married, but when his wife discovered that he slept in a wigwam on a bearskin run, she insisted that he build them a cabin with a proper bed.

Jacob continued to live a life of adventure, acting as a spy during a conflict with the Shawnee, and then serving for the Patriots in the American Revolution from 1782–1785. Jacob's log cabin still stands in Alleghany County, Virginia, and is a National Historical landmark.[75]

Part 3: Ancestors of Don Thomas

Don's ancestors have generally been traced back to the mid 1700s. To put into context the times and issues of the world that his ancestors knew, the following timelines show key milestones in the nation's history, and some of Don's ancestors who lived during those times.

Don's most distant known ancestor in the Thomas line, John Thomas, would have heard about the American Revolution from his home in England. As a young boy in England, James Thomas Sr. may have heard about a Gold Rush in a faraway place called California. Years later, young James Thomas Jr. may have been fascinated to hear about an amazing invention called the telephone. Both father and son came to America in 1884, before the Statue Of Liberty was there to welcome immigrants.

The Civil War had been over for about ten years when Mary Edelen was born, though the aftermath of the war would take much longer to sort out. The Ford Model T was introduced when William "Tommy" Thomas was a young boy, but like many others, he would face very hard times in the Great Depression as a young adult.

Marjorie Hill worried about her family in England during World War II, and apparently tried to support her native country with both money and goods.

Now, many years later, I use the Internet, a tool my ancestors could not have possibly imagined, to research their lives and times.

Figure 9. Timeline - Don Thomas Ancestors to 1800

1400's	1500-1550	1550-1600	1600-1650	1650-1700	1700-1750	1750-1800
• Columbus discovers America	• Accession of Henry VIII (England) • DeLeon explores Florida • Cabrilo enters California	• Drake enters San Francisco Bay • First English Colony in America	• English settlement at Jamestown • First Thanksgiving • King James Bible completed	• English capture "New York" from Dutch • Philadelphia named • London plague & fire	• Ben Franklin publishes "Poor Richard's Almanac" • Baltimore founded	• Industrial Revolution • Declaration of Independence • Revolutionary War • Washington 1st President

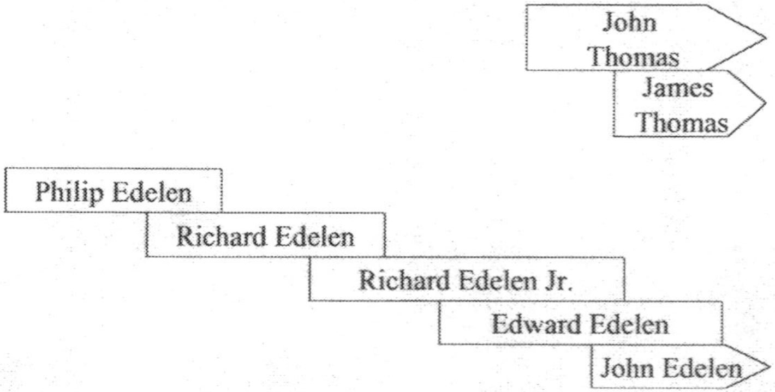

John Thomas

James Thomas

Philip Edelen

Richard Edelen

Richard Edelen Jr.

Edward Edelen

John Edelen

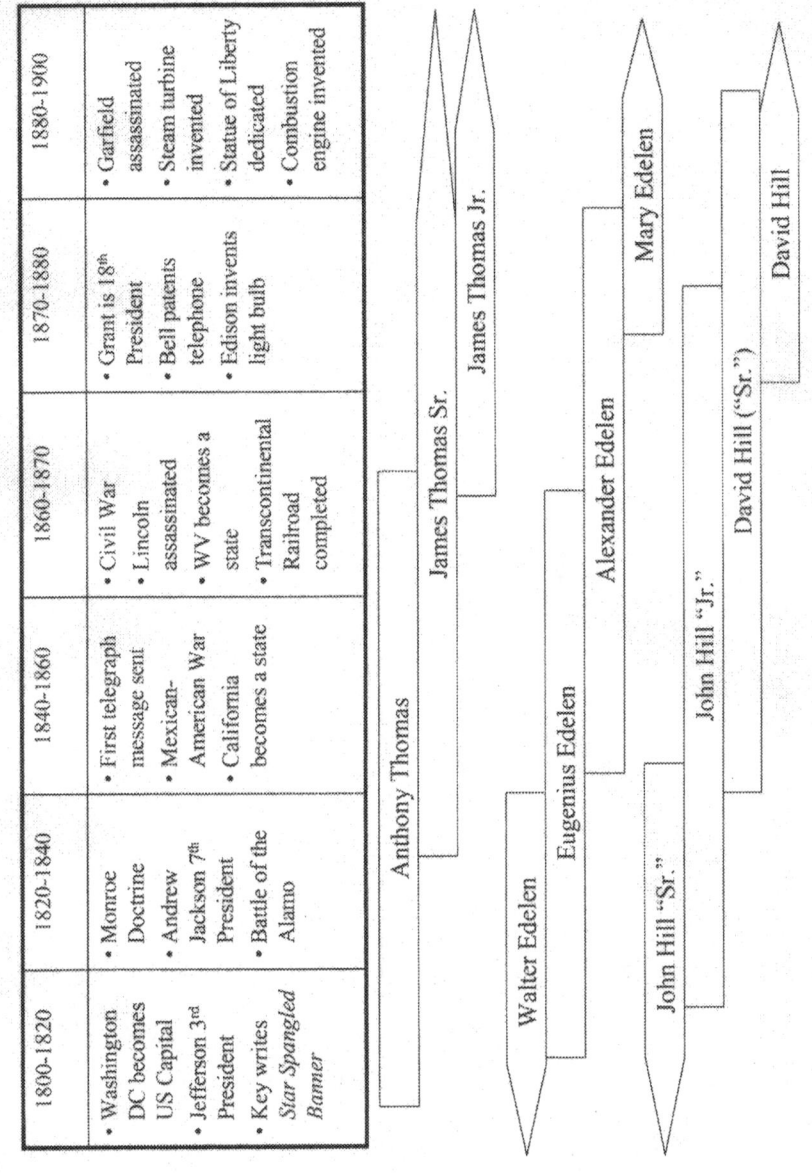

Figure 10. Timeline - Don Thomas Ancestors 1800-1900

1800-1820	1820-1840	1840-1860	1860-1870	1870-1880	1880-1900
• Washington DC becomes US Capital • Jefferson 3rd President • Key writes *Star Spangled Banner*	• Monroe Doctrine • Andrew Jackson 7th President • Battle of the Alamo	• First telegraph message sent • Mexican-American War • California becomes a state	• Civil War • Lincoln assassinated • WV becomes a state • Transcontinental Railroad completed	• Grant is 18th President • Bell patents telephone • Edison invents light bulb	• Garfield assassinated • Steam turbine invented • Statue of Liberty dedicated • Combustion engine invented

Anthony Thomas

James Thomas Sr.

James Thomas Jr.

Walter Edelen

Eugenius Edelen

Alexander Edelen

Mary Edelen

John Hill "Sr."

John Hill "Jr."

David Hill ("Sr.")

David Hill

Figure 11. Timeline - Don Thomas Ancestors 1900-1970

1900-1910	1910-1920	1920-1930	1930-1940	1940-1950	1950-1960	1960-1970
• Teddy Roosevelt is 26th President • Wright Brothers flight • Ford introduces Model T	• Titanic sinks • World War I • Panama Canal opens	• Women's Suffrage • Roaring Twenties • Lindberg's transatlantic flight • Stock Market crash	• Great Depression • FDR President	• Pearl Harbor • World War II • Atomic age	• Korean War • Cold War	• JFK assassinated • Vietnam War • Man walks on the Moon

James Thomas Jr.

William R. Thomas

David Hill

Marjorie Hill

Mary Edelen

Don Thomas & Reba Martin

DON'S PARENTS

Don's father, and my grandfather, was **William R. "Tommy" Thomas**, born in 1899 in Washington D.C.[76]

Growing up in the nation's capital provided some interesting moments. One day Tommy encountered President William Howard Taft (who served from 1909–1913) and his Secret Service detail, who were all walking toward him on the boardwalk. To Tommy's surprise, President Taft, who was a huge man, and his entire entourage all got off the boardwalk to let young Tommy walk by!

Tommy was educated through high school, attending McKinley Tech, which was apparently a military school in D.C.[77] He just missed being of age to serve in World War I, though interestingly he never mentioned anything about it to his son Don. As a young man he worked as a vendor at baseball games of the old Washington Senators, many times getting to see the legendary Walter Johnson pitch.[78]

William "Tommy" Thomas (third from left) and friends, c1920.

Tommy lost his father when he was 18, and apparently went to work in order to help support the family. In 1920, Tommy was working as a draftsman for the Maryland archives.[79] Perhaps after this he worked at a water plant at Riverdale, and then the Hyattsville sanitation department in Maryland.[80] Sometime around 1925 he went to Cleveland for a job as an engineer at HK Ferguson, a chemical and engineering company.

Note that in addition to the photos shown here, another picture of Tommy as a young man is included on the cover of this book (fourth row, second from left).

William "Tommy" Thomas, probably while at work at the Maryland Archives, c1920.

During the late twenties and early thirties, the family moved several times. They apparently lived in New York with Aunt Doris (sister of Tommy's wife), and then lived in Baltimore in 1930.[81] Next was a move to Asheville, North Carolina, and then back to Cleveland.[82]

Unfortunately, this was the time of the Great Depression. Tommy lost his job with HK Ferguson, and eventually moved back to Washington D.C. to live with his mother. He apparently had a variety of jobs as he tried to support his family, including a job as a "soda jerk," where he mixed drinks like coca-cola and made milkshakes at a soda fountain. The family stayed in Washington D.C. until the early 1930s.

Looking for work in those hard times, Tommy heard of an opening for a 3–6 month job at Union Carbide, a chemical company in Charleston West Virginia. His wife told him to take the family savings, which was about $16, and to go to Charleston to pursue the job. He went to Charleston in 1934, got the job for six months, and parlayed that into a 28-year career with Carbide!

Initially the family lived in an apartment across the street from the State Capitol in Charleston, and as of 2003 this apartment building still stood. For most of their years in West Virginia, the family lived at 1016 Highland Drive in St. Albans.

Don recalls how his father had to scrap to get a job and provide for his family during the Depression. "The only college he went to was correspondence school, but I think to get his job, or to hold his job, he claimed he was a college graduate. His boss probably knew the truth, but never said anything about it. He did what he had to do in those days to get a job and support his family."

Tommy considered joining the military in WWII, but concluded that to match the income he had from his job at Carbide that he'd have to go in as a major, and he assumed the military was unlikely to give him a major's commission.

"He was responsible for the design and installation of the water treatment facilities at all of Carbide's chemical plants," says Don. "He traveled around a fair amount, mainly to Texas City and Seadrift, to visit Carbide's plants."

"My father was sort of my ideal, even more today than at the time," recalls Don. "As a kid I just didn't recognize all that he did for me. I appreciate him vastly more today, because of all the sacrifices he and my mother made for me. He was a very positive person, and never lost his temper. He smiled a lot, and never said anything negative about anything or anybody."

His pride and joy: William "Tommy" Thomas tending bar at his home in St. Albans WV, c1966

After taking early retirement from Union Carbide, Tommy became manager of the St. Albans Water and Sewer department, and worked there until 1967. Around 1970 Tommy retired to Cape Coral, Florida, and enjoyed his hobbies of fishing, photography, and stamp collecting. He died in Cape Coral in 1975.

Don's mother, **Marjorie Hill**, was born in London in 1900. She came to the U.S. in 1910, and her family settled in the Black Hills of South Dakota. Native American Indians lived in wigwams at the bottom of the hill by their house, and would sometimes seek shelter with the family during violent storms.

Marjorie's father worked as a custodian at the State Capitol during her teenage years. Probably through her father's job, her best friend as a teenager was the governor's daughter, and through this friend she was able to attend a dinner for President Taft at the South Dakota governors mansion.[83] It is remarkable that both Marjorie Hill and Tommy Thomas would personally encounter President Taft as children.

By 1920, the Hill family had moved to Cleveland, and Marjorie worked there as a stenographer.[84]

Tommy and Marjorie apparently met when Tommy came on as a boarder at the Hill home in Cleveland. They married in 1927 in Cleveland, and had two children, Don and Jean.[85]

When World War II broke out in 1939 in Europe, Marjorie "was very upset, and worried about her family still in England," says her daughter Jean. "In the years to come, she headed efforts to raise money and send items to England. We knitted sweaters to go into 'Bundles for Britain' for the RAF, and we knitted for the Red Cross. Mother gave Teas to raise money for the cause, though it was difficult to do with the rationing."[86]

Marjorie kept house, and was active in the Episcopal Church and the local woman's club. She enjoyed sewing and hosting family dinners.

"She was a housewife, and a very nice person," says Don of his mother. "She never lost her temper, and she was utterly devoted to Dad. If anybody said anything about him, she defended him like a lion."

Just before she died, Marjorie instructed that she was to be buried with her wedding rings. She passed away in 1963, and is buried in St. Albans, West Virginia.

Marjorie Hill's engagement picture, c1927.

After Marjorie's death, William Thomas married **Judith "Jackie" Vandyne**. Jackie was born 1913.

Tommy and Jackie moved into another house in St. Albans just down the street from the house where Tommy had previously lived, and I remember how their new home was the destination for many genteel hikes that my father and I would make. Our regular route was to walk along the railroad tracks for a mile or two, then up a hill to a big rock, upon which we'd rest, admire the valley below, and have a snack. Our snack was usually an oatmeal cake, and thus we unofficially christened our resting spot "Oatmeal Rock." We'd then hike up and over the small hill, exiting on Highland Drive, where we walked a half-mile or so to "Papa and Jackie's," where I would be treated to a cold root beer. Then my mother would pick us up in the car and drive us home. A very genteel hike indeed!

After Tommy's death in 1975, Jackie stayed in Cape Coral, Florida, and did office work for an insurance company. She later moved to Chattanooga, Tennessee in 1995, to be closer to Don and Reba. A very kind woman, Jackie died in 1997.

Tommy's second wife, Jackie Vandine, c1980.

Jackie's family was from Sissonville, West Virginia. Her father, Otis Vandine, was born around 1887. He was a Poca District Justice of the Peace and also served as a court bailiff. He died in 1963.

Jackie's mother was Maggie Vandine, born around 1883. At one time Maggie worked as a saleswoman at the Diamond department store in Charleston. She died in 1953.[87]

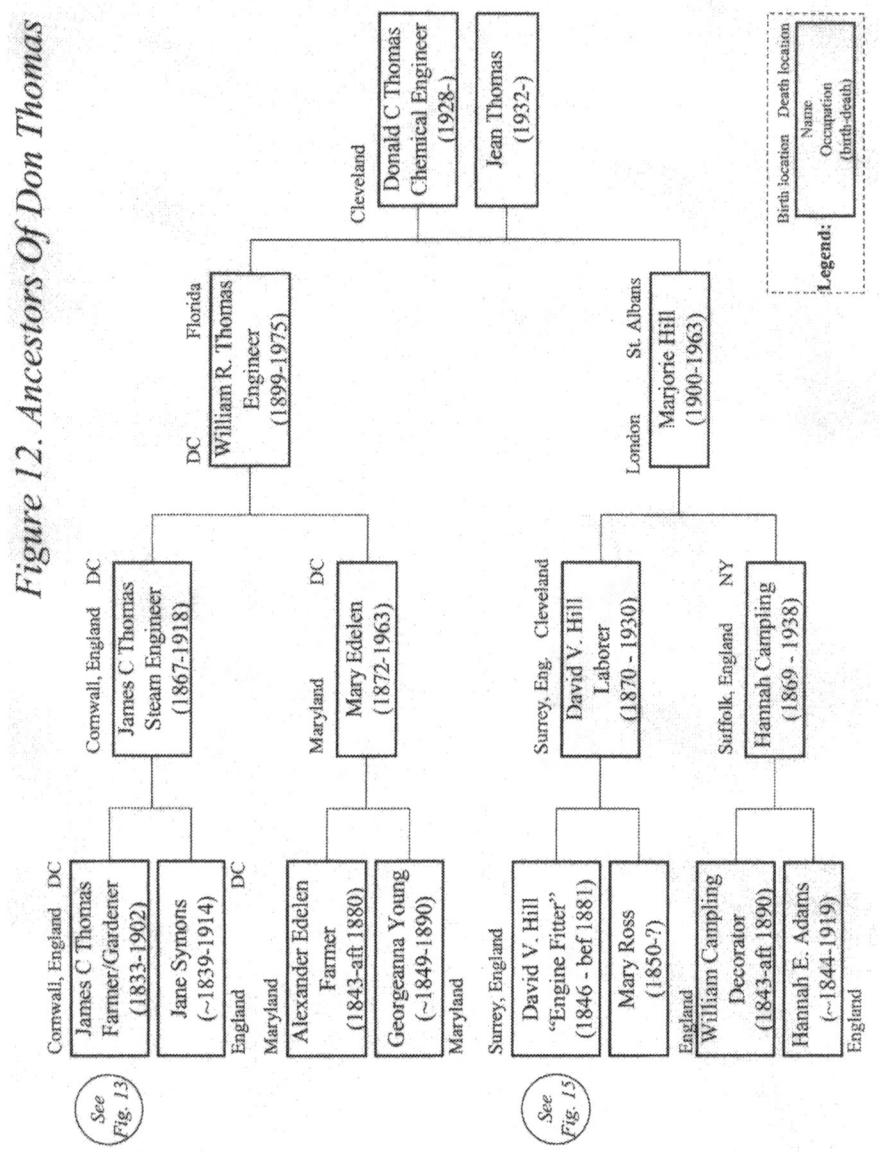

Figure 12. Ancestors Of Don Thomas

THE THOMAS LINE

Tommy's father, **James C. Thomas**, was born in 1867, in Mylor, Cornwall County, England. He grew up in Cornwall, and was 17 when his father brought the eleven members of the family to the U.S. in 1884.

Two months after arriving in the U.S., James enrolled for a one-year stint on the U.S. Navy ship *Albatross.*[88] His job on the Albatross was listed as "fireman," which implies that he tended the fire on the ship. The Albatross was a Marine research ship, and sailed up and down the East Coast on various research projects. While James was on board in 1884–85 the ship made forays to Maine, New Orleans, and the Bahamas, for activities such as examining tilefish grounds, studying red snapper, and studying the impacts of the Gulf Stream on bottom-feeders.[89] However, with his job of keeping coal in the fire, it's possible that James did not see much of the scenery.

James Thomas (front row, first on left), assumed on the Albatross, c1885

As of the 1900 census, James and his wife Mary were living with his brother Samuel (and Samuel's wife Catherine), just a few blocks away from his parents.

Later, he listed his occupation as "steam engineer," and for many years he was the engineer responsible for running the equipment in the Washington Monument in Washington D.C.

James Thomas at work at the Washington Monument, early 1900's.

James worked at the Washington Monument until he died in 1918. Family lore is that he died in the Influenza epidemic (see below), but this may be incorrect. The catastrophic outbreak of Influenza in 1918 is believed to have started with the first known cases on March 11 in Kansas, so it would seem unlikely that James died from this in Washington just three days later.

On March 15, 1918, the front page of the *Washington Post* was filled with stories about World War I. On page 3 under "DEATHS" was the notice for James Thomas:

THOMAS-Entered eternal life on Thursday, March 14, 1918, at his residence, 124 Eleventh Street Southeast, JAMES C., beloved husband of Mary C. Thomas. Funeral at the Nativity Chapel, Fourteenth and A Streets Southeast, Saturday, March 16, at 230PM. Interment at Congressional Cemetery.

The Worst Epidemic In Human History

The 1918 flu virus was perhaps the worst infectious disease outbreak in the history of mankind. Known at the time as the "Spanish Flu," in 1918 it killed a total of some 675,000 Americans, and between 20 and 50 million people worldwide. The virus is believed to have started at an American army base in the Midwest, and then spread to Europe via soldiers going over for World War I. Many victims died in just a few days. The epidemic exploded in the fall of 1918, with 195,000 Americans dying in October alone. In November, when some 30,000 people assembled in San Francisco to celebrate the end of World War I, virtually all of them wore face-masks.[90]

James married Tommy's mother, **Mary Cornelia "Nealie" Edelen**, in 1898.[91] She had been born in 1872 in Maryland, apparently in Prince George's County, which borders Washington D.C.[92] Her father was a farmer, but she did not like living in "the country," and when her mother died young, she moved from Maryland to Washington D.C. and lived with an aunt. At some point she worked as a saleslady for Kamn's department store.

Things were very tough after her husband James died in 1918, as Mary was now a widow with five children. "She took in boarders to make some money," says her daughter Elizabeth Goodnight, "So that she didn't have to put us kids in an orphanage." Her boarders were primarily government employees, and for example in her 1920 census she listed six boarders in the house, in addition to her children. Elizabeth briefly stayed with Uncle Harry who had a farm in Falls Church, and the kids worked as soon as they were able. Apparently it was very tough, but she got by.[93]

Mary Edelen Thomas, mother of William Thomas, c1923.

The Thomas family bought a house around 1894 in Washington D.C. at 124 Eleventh St. SE, and Nealie lived there for some 60 years. Note that an additional photo of Nealie is included on the cover of this book (bottom row, third from left).

Nealie died in 1963, at the age of 91.[94] She was buried at Congressional Cemetery in Washington D.C. Her brother Guy, who served in WWI, is buried at Arlington National Cemetery.[95]

In addition to William, James and Mary had four other children. James Jr. (~1904–abt 1980?) became a mechanic and worked in a garage. The three girls in the family all remained in the Washington area. Helen (~1902–?) married Perry Beckley, Florence (b. ~1909) married Harvey Lawrenson in 1935, and in 1945

Elizabeth (b. 1916) married Harlan Goodnight. Florence and Elizabeth are currently living in Silver Spring, MD.

The Thomas Family, c1906
Back Row *(L-R): Harry, Sam, Richard, Jack "John," James (father of Tommy)*
Middle Row*: Mary (mother of Tommy), Katie (wife of Sam), Flora (wife of Richard), Mary (sister of James), Jane Symons (grandmother of Tommy), Mame (wife of Jack), Elizabeth "Bess" (sister of James)*
Front Row*: James (son of James), Helen (daughter of James), Vivien (daughter of Sam), William "Tommy" Thomas, Russell (son of Jack).*

A few tidbits are known about James' siblings shown in the above photo. Sam had an auto repair shop, in what would have been the early days of the automobile. Both Harry and Bess worked for the U.S. Government, perhaps at the Bureau of Engraving and Printing, and lived at Harry's farm in Virginia. Mary had severe rheumatism, and was an invalid for much of her life. Jack worked at Barber & Ross in Washington, and Richard liked to play the horses.[96]

The father of James Cornish Thomas was also named **James Cornish Thomas**. The elder James was born in 1833 at Falmouth, Cornwall County, England.

In 1865 James married **Jane Symons** (Simmons), who was born around 1839 at St. Neot, in Cornwall. James worked as a miner at the time of his marriage, but later would become a farmer.

James and Jane would have more than their share of tragedy, with only 8 of their 13 children surviving until 1900, and with family lore suggesting that James lost a substantial sum in a bank failure.

James lived and farmed at several locations, including Falmouth, Mylor and then St. Austell, all in the same general area in Cornwall County.

Falmouth in the 1880s

Bob Richards, a Cornwall genealogist who has researched the Thomas line on my behalf, tells us what it was like in Falmouth in the 1880s:

By the 1880s, Falmouth had already been a busy port for shipping for several hundred years. Its geographical location on the far west of England and its large deepwater harbor made it an ideal location for an expanding shipping service to all parts of the World. As it was the first enclosed bay for ships arriving from the west, and the last enclosed bay for ships leaving England, it had long been a strategically significant location.

From as early as 1689, "Falmouth Packet" ships were plying their trade across the ever-expanding known World. These were small vessels, lightly armed and built for speed rather than standing to fight with any would-be enemy on the high seas. They were operated by the Postal service but as well as mail and news from foreign parts, they also carried light cargo. The expression "Falmouth for Orders" was well known in shipping circles.

It was possible for a ship to leave the Port of London and sail down the channel to Falmouth, weather permitting, in about four or five days. The journey in the other direction took about a day shorter on average because of prevailing winds. It took a man on a horse about a day or two less to do the same journey and so ships called at Falmouth both inward and outward bound to receive any last minute orders or changes to orders from their owners in London and other places and to give news of their arrival and their cargoes. By the 1850's many trade and post routes were established to and from Falmouth.

Before steamships became prevalent in the 1800s, the duration of the journeys to other continents was very long. Falmouth to Halifax, Nova

Scotia, on to Bermuda and home via Madeira was a trip which averaged some 78 days, although the record was just 44. Falmouth to Buenos Aires via Rio de Janeiro and other South American ports was a round trip of almost 6 months. Imagine then the joy, relief and cause for celebration when one of these ships came home, as they did on a regular basis and the clambering for news of relatives who might be now in Mexico or Canada or elsewhere earning a living from mining now that the Cornish tin and copper mines were closing fast. These Packet Ships had regular and specific timetables, for example, Lisbon was served weekly, and there was monthly service to Virginia, the West Indies and Mexico. New York was also monthly and, except in winter when icebergs were a problem, this service also called at Halifax, Nova Scotia.

Even into the 1880s, shipwrecks were a common item on the front page of the local newspaper, "The Falmouth Packet." Ships were regularly reported lost, or arriving in port with enormous damage from the rough seas.

With the shipping industry and it's attendant land-based occupations and as well as its own thriving fishing fleet, Falmouth was indeed a lively and bustling port in the 19th century. It had always been of strategic importance fending off the likes of Napoleon, but in the 1800s the port was at its peak. Its harbor entrance was still guarded by two castles from the time of the English Civil War.

To support such a thriving shipping industry there was an obvious need for all and sundry trades to develop, not only directly associated with boat building, the sea and ships but also to feed, clothe, entertain and generally see to the well-being of the place. Farms grew up around the town and brought their produce to regular markets. Drapers, Butchers, Bakers, Fish merchants, Grocers, China and Glass merchants, Bookshops, Hotels, Boarding houses and any number of other trades are to be found here serving the resident population and its many temporary visitors from all corners of the World. There was even one shop towards the end of the 19th century called "Burton's Old Curiosity Shop" in Market Street which promised that, given time, it could supply anything from anywhere in the World. Its windows were packed with all manner of odd objects and for many years the jawbone of a whale stood outside, said to be an uncollected order from a customer.

There was also poverty. Many thousands of Cornish miners were thrown out of work when cheaper ore was discovered in the New World of North and South America, Australia, New Zealand and South Africa among other places in the 19th century and as a result, those who did not emigrate to find new work often drifted into the towns only to find poverty and no prospect of work.

Small, squalid and overcrowded houses down to the water's edge of the inner harbor were in stark contrast to the new houses being built for the merchants, sea captains and others on the higher ground overlooking the main town. Other fine buildings were also to be found in the town, the Customs House, a busy place with all the shipping activity, the Falmouth Subscription Rooms, a very "up-market" Gentleman's Club and others were designed and built in this era, some with classical Greek style portico and columns.

As well as the traditional Church of England Parish Church and the Methodist Chapel there was a Roman Catholic place of Worship and others including a Seamen's Mission, tending to the spiritual needs of visiting sailors of all nationalities. Its pulpit was in the form of a ship's bow, complete with wheel, anchor chains and rail.

Education was not forgotten. The 19th century saw numerous schools opened in Falmouth and other places giving free education to everyone under new Acts of Parliament. Some of these buildings still survive today, as schools and now often converted to other uses. The first Falmouth Hospital was built around the year 1893 and also in the second half of the 19th century sports teams playing Cricket, Football, Rugby and Tennis were to be found in the town.

The railway had come to Falmouth in 1863, a direct route from London taking in the vast ports of Bristol and Plymouth on the way down. This brought it's own new industry, tourists. Instead of the three days by road coach from London, the journey could now be done in less than a day. This led directly to a group of local businessmen building the Falmouth Hotel on the strip of land between the main harbor and the beaches. Other Hotels giving top-flight accommodation to the new tourist industry also began to emerge and tourism eventually took over from shipping as the main industry of the town.

It is not known why James Thomas decided to bring his family to the U.S., but certainly an exodus from Cornwall was underway. Cornwall had traditionally been a center for mining of tin and copper, but by 1850 huge deposits of tin and copper had been found abroad, and those deposits were often more accessible than the deep mines of Cornwall. Thus, from 1850–1900 Cornwall lost some 25% of it's population, as her residents left for the U.S., Australia, New Zealand, South America, and South Africa.[97] Other common complaints of the time were high taxes, expensive land, and a general lack of opportunity. Any or all of these factors may have led James Thomas to seek a better future in America.

James brought his family to the U.S. on the ship *Italy*, which sailed from London on April 23, 1884, arriving in New York two weeks later on May 7. The Thomas family clearly traveled on a meager budget, as the "National Line" that ran the *Italy* was the lowest-priced steamship line advertised in *The Times* Of London, and the Thomas family traveled in steerage (third class). The cost of passage was four British Pounds per person. The 11 family members brought with them a total of only 5 pieces of luggage for their start in the New World.[98]

Though they arrived in New York, the family would not have been welcomed with a view of the Statue Of Liberty, as in 1884 the statue was still under construction in Paris. They also would not have been processed at famed Ellis Island, which did not open until 1892. It is assumed that they were instead processed at a facility called Castle Garden, at the tip of Southern Manhattan in what is now Battery Park.

When immigrants arrived at Castle Island, they would either connect to their final destination (typically via train), have family or friends to pick them up, or wait at the Castle Island facility until they had arranged a job. It is not known how or why James Thomas settled in Washington D.C.

Coming To America: The Immigrant's Experience

When James Thomas sailed to the United States in 1884, the trip was no longer the horrific experience that it had been for Johann Roush in 1750 (see earlier section). With the advent of steam-powered travel, the trip from England to New York was cut from 40 days to two weeks. However, it still was not an easy or pleasant process, particularly for those who traveled in steerage class, as the Thomas family did.

Prior to boarding the ship in England, immigrants were first put through a health inspection. Passengers were then separated and taken to their respective areas of the ship. First class was known as "saloon class," and depending on the ship, accommodations ranged from acceptable to elegant.

Steerage, or third class, was in the hold of the ship, and was far less pleasant. Sleeping was done in bunks strung perhaps three-high, usually consisting of a piece of fabric strung between two steel pipes. Eating was communal, with steerage passengers serving themselves from a tureen of soup or stew. There was no privacy, and for the majority of the voyage steerage passengers were stuck in a hot, stuffy, stinking hold. In heavy seas, steerage could become a hellish place, with dozens or hundreds of passengers screaming in panic as the ship was tossed. Any rough seas may have been a particular problem on James' voyage, as the relatively small number of passengers (about 50 people in saloon class, and 179 in steerage) may suggest that the *Italy* was a relatively small ship.[99]

In Washington, James worked as a gardener, and gained U.S. citizenship in 1895, but nothing else is known of his life in the U.S.

James died in 1902, and his wife Jane died in 1914. Both are buried in the Old Congressional Cemetery in Washington D.C.[100]

Figure 13. Ancestors Of James Thomas *

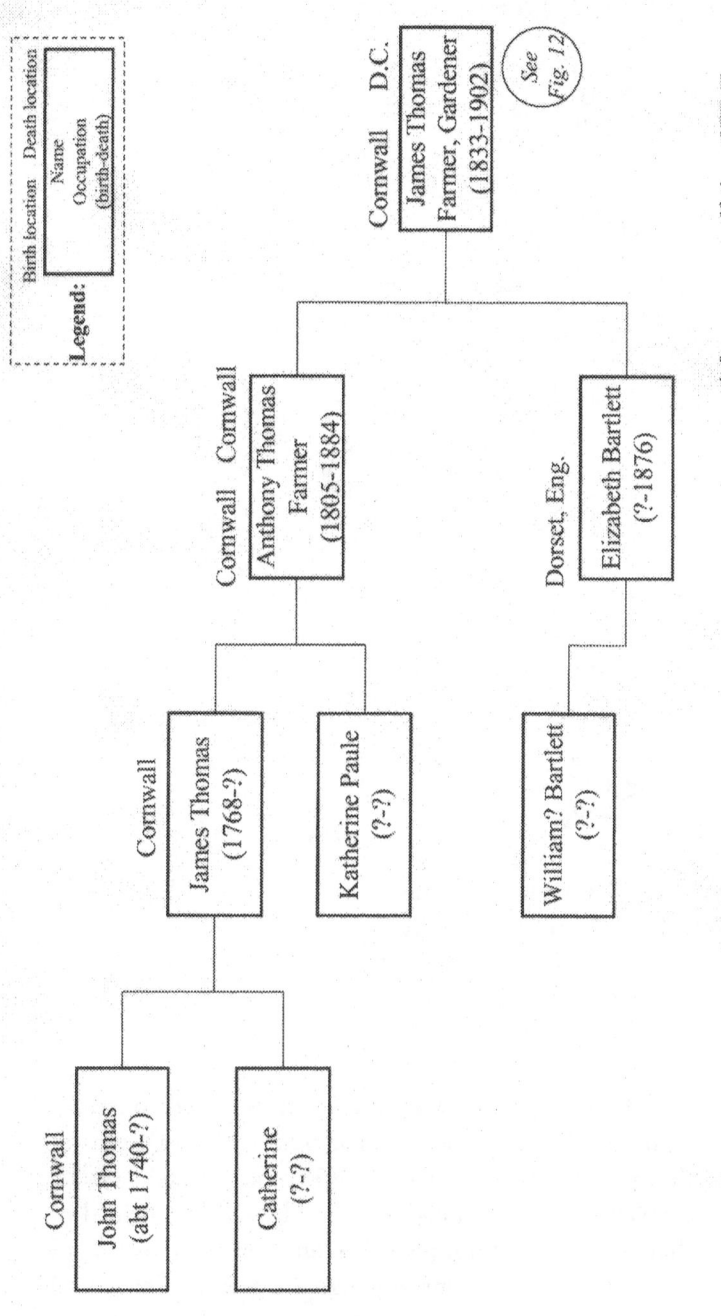

Figure 14. Ancestral Homes In England

Hannah Campling (mother of Marjorie Hill) and her ancestors hailed from Suffolk County

London

David Hill (father of Marjorie Hill) and his ancestors were from Surrey County

The ancestors of William R "Tommy" Thomas lived in Cornwall County

James was the son of **Anthony Thomas** and **Elizabeth Bartlett**. Anthony was born in 1805 in St. Gluvias, which is an ancient parish in Cornwall. For most of his life Anthony was a farmer. In the 1850's he worked 100 acres of land in Budock, Cornwall County, and had nine employees who helped run the farm. It is believed that Anthony did not own this land, but was instead a tenant farmer. Interestingly, this land lay adjacent to where the grand Falmouth Hotel would be built in 1865. The Falmouth Hotel remains, to this day, one of the better hotels in Cornwall.

Anthony and Elizabeth had at least eight children, though two of the children died while they were very young. Their daughter Catherine married a man with the last name of Worden, and around 1859 the couple had their son Joseph Worden in South Australia. It is not known what Catherine was doing in South Australia, though around this time there was substantial migration from Cornwall to many other parts of the world. Two years later, Catherine and her son were back in Cornwall, but nothing else is known of her husband, or whether she remained in Cornwall.

By 1871, Anthony was an innkeeper at the Central Hotel in Falmouth. The Central Hotel still stands, and is close to the docks and ship repair yards, where Anthony's son Richard (a shipwright) likely worked.

Elizabeth Bartlett was born in Weymouth, which is another port town some 200 miles up the English Channel to the east, in the County of Dorset.

Five months after his son James had left for the United States, Anthony died in Falmouth on September 27, 1884.

The parents of Anthony Thomas were **James Thomas** and his wife **Katherine Paule**. James was probably born around 1768.[101] Nothing is known of him, except for an indication that he could not read or write, as he did not sign his marriage certificate, but rather made a "mark" which was witnessed.

James in turn is believed to have been the son of **John Thomas** and his wife **Catherine**. John was probably born around 1740, and this is as far back as the Thomas line has been reliably traced.

All of these Thomas ancestors lived in the area around Falmouth, in Cornwall County, England, but otherwise nothing is known about their lives.

THE EDELEN LINE

Nealie Edelen's ancestors had lived in Maryland since the 1660's.

Nealie was the daughter of **Alexander Edelen** (1843–aft. 1880) and **Georgiana Young** (1849–1890), who married in 1867[102]. Alexander was a farmer.

Alexander Edelen, *father of Mary Edelen*

Alexander was son of **Eugenius Edelen** (1812–aft 1864) and his wife **Ellen**.

Eugenius was son of **Walter Edelen** (?–1842) and wife **Louisa Gardiner** (~1791–aft 1870), who married in 1811.

Walter was son of **John Edelen** (?–1803) and **Monica Boarman**[103] (?–aft 1803). Records indicate that John had nine children, and was active in various land deals in the 1780s and 1790s. His personal holdings as of his death in 1803 were valued at roughly $2600, and among his estate were numerous slaves that he bequeathed to his wife Monica.

John was son of **Edward Edelen** (1717–1780) and **Susanah Wathan** (?–aft 1780). John received from his father some 730 acres of land in Charles County, and he and his wife had 13 children.

Edward was son of **Richard Edelen Jr.** (1671–1760) and **Sara Hagan**. Edward was an architect and builder, which were responsibilities that then fell under the title of "carpenter." Richard and Sara were parents of at least eight children.

Richard was son of **Richard Edelen Sr.** (1635–1694) and wife **Elizabeth Banton**. Richard was the original Edelen immigrant ancestor, moving from London to St. Mary's County, Maryland around 1664.

The Interesting History Of Prince George's County

In 1632, King Charles I of England ceded the land that was to become Maryland to Cecil Calvert, second Lord Baltimore, and settlers soon arrived in Prince George's County. The land had until then been inhabited by two Indian tribes: the Piscataways and the Susquehannocks. By the time Richard Edelen arrived in 1664 there were probably a few hundred settlers, and by 1696 the settler population was around two thousand people.

Tobacco became the lifeblood of Prince George's County. The tobacco trade generated substantial wealth, and a sophisticated society developed complete with grand plantation homes, theatre, and thoroughbred horse racing.

After the Revolution, Prince George's County ceded much of the land that would comprise Washington D.C. The County was later in the middle of the action during the War of 1812, and the British marched through Prince George's on their way to burning Washington D.C. On the way back to their ships, the British captured Prince George's resident Dr. William Beanes. Francis Scott Key was sent to negotiate for the release of Dr. Beanes, and it was on this visit that Key saw the battle at Fort McHenry and wrote the poem that would later become the Star Spangled Banner.

The tobacco industry was built on the back on slave labor, and by the Civil War, slaves accounted for 60% of the population. When my great-grandmother Mary Edelen was born in 1872, there were a great many freed slaves who worked and even operated some of the tobacco farms. At the time of Mary's birth, Washington D.C. was essentially a town, but in the coming years it would grow into a major city, and would have the effect of transforming Prince George's County from a tobacco-based economy to a suburban center supporting the Nation's Capital.[104]

Richard returned to England in 1665, but was then back in Maryland by 1667. His travels back and forth would seem to suggest that he was affluent, and his trip may or may not have also been related to two catastrophic events of that time, the Great London Fire and the outbreak of Bubonic Plague (see below).

Richard and his wife Elizabeth settled in St. Mary's County, Maryland, where they initially had 100 acres of land, and where Richard worked as a surveyor.[105] It is documented that he participated in an Assembly meeting in 1688, and for his work received 1200 pounds of tobacco. Richard was also a carpenter, and apparently built many fine homes, several of which still stand today.

The maiden name of Richard's first wife was Neale, and it's possible that Mary Edelen's middle name of Cornelia may reflect this was name was carried down through the generations.

Richard was the son of **Philip Edelen** (~1598–1656), a minister in the Church of England, who attended Cambridge University.

London—A Bad Place To Visit in 1665

Bubonic Plague had been around in the British Islands since the 1300's. However, in 1665, apparently while Richard Edelen was visiting his native country, a horrific outbreak of plague engulfed London. Initially starting in the spring of 1665 in the poorer sections of London, by summer the epidemic was in full force. The Lord Mayor closed the gates of the city, and only those who possessed a health certificate were permitted to leave. Understandably, a black market for forged health certificates quickly developed.

In July the Lord Mayor had all cats and dogs destroyed, as it was believed that these were the animals that spread plague. In actuality this likely made matters much worse, as now there were no cats to kill the rats that hosted the fleas which we now know spread the disease. If someone in a household caught plague, then guards were posted outside the house and nobody could either come or go for 40 days.

By August, the death rate was roughly 6000 people per week, and only with the onset of winter would the rate substantially decrease. As many as 100,000 people may have died during the epidemic that finally ended in the spring of 1666.

However, London was in store for yet another catastrophe. In September 1666, a small fire started, and quickly spread through the densely developed city of wooden buildings. Some 13,000 homes burned, and 15% of the population was left homeless.

THE HILL LINE

Marjorie's father, **David Hill**, was born in 1870 in Surrey County, England, just outside London. David's father died relatively young, perhaps before David reached the age of ten.

David married **Hannah "Annie" Campling** in 1890.[106] As of 1891 they were living in London with Annie's uncle. At the time David listed his occupation as "clerk," and he is believed to have been in the scrap iron business in England.

David immigrated to the U.S. in 1908, arriving in New York with his oldest daughter Mildred. This was some 24 years after James Thomas came to the U.S., and at this time David Hill would have been welcomed by a view of the Statue Of Liberty, and probably would have been processed at Ellis Island.[107]

The *St. Paul*

David Hill came to America on the *St. Paul*, an ocean liner in service of American Lines. The St. Paul was some 550 feet long, and could carry 1340 passengers.

Interestingly, this ship had briefly been in the fleet of the U.S. Navy as an auxiliary cruiser during the Spanish-American war. In April 1908, a few months before David sailed on the same ship, the *St. Paul* had collided with the *HMS Gladiator* during a storm in Liverpool, resulting in the deaths of 27 people.[108]

It is believed that David had a job lined-up in New York, perhaps at a steamship company. However, he loved horses and heard that there were lots of them out west, so he went to South Dakota. He settled in Pierre, South Dakota, and was later joined by his wife and their other two children in 1910.[109] In 1915, he indicated that his occupation was "fireman and engineer."

Somewhere along the line David may have been injured in an accident. It is believed that at some point he was hit in the head with a shovel, and it is said that afterwards he was never the same.[110]

David Hill's Declaration of Intent for U.S. Citizenship, 1911.

David Hill (1913) and wife Annie Campling.
Photos courtesy of David Ferguson.

In 1913–14, David was a janitor at the State Capitol. He liked opera, played the piano at home, and played the organ at the local Episcopal Church.[111] The day World War I ended, he was taking delivery of a piano for the family home, and as the piano sat outside, he played "Over There!" to the joy of all around.

Sometime around 1918 he moved the family to Cleveland, Ohio. As of 1920 David worked as an assembler at a manufacturing company, and as of 1930 he was Night Watchman at the Cleveland Club.[112]

David Hill died in Cleveland in 1930, and is buried at Lake View Cemetery in Cleveland. Coincidentally, both John D. Rockefeller and U.S. President James Garfield are also buried at Lake View.[113]

David's wife Annie, born around 1867, was said to be "very spirited."[114] After David died, Annie lived with her daughter Peggy in the Virgin Islands. It was there that she "introduced" one of her grandchildren, David Ferguson, to President Franklin D. Roosevelt. FDR was going by in a parade, as the story goes, and Annie was there along with a maid who was carrying David. As FDR was going by, Annie asked "which one of you is the President?" to which FDR replied "I am!" Annie then waved young David's hand to Roosevelt, who kindly waved back.[115]

Annie died in 1938 in New York City, and is buried with her husband at Lake View Cemetery in Cleveland.[116]

In addition to Marjorie, David and Hannah had four other children, Mildred, Doris, Maud, and Billy.

Mildred (b. 1894) was also known as "Peggy," and was gifted in the arts. One of her paintings has hung in the homes of Tommy Thomas, and then Donald Thomas, to this day. During WWII she lived at the Albert Hotel in New York, and later she married Karl Root, who was collector of customs in St. Thomas, Virgin Islands.

Doris (b. 1898) led a very active life. She left Cleveland as a young lady, and went to New York with a total of $50. Things were tough in New York, and she approached a well-off family from Cleveland, the Hesses, to see if they had any work for her. For her meeting with the Hess family she blackened her stockings so that the holes in her shoes wouldn't show.

Doris had a variety of jobs from New York to Michigan to Miami. She was a case worker at the welfare department, a travelers aid at Penn Central station (where she happened to meet Eleanor Roosevelt), established a foster home program, ran a YWCA, helped manage a hotel, and eventually was in charge of facilities, catering and the art gallery at Finch College in New York City.

Doris was said to be tough but fair, and an example comes from the Great Depression. During this time, several lawyers who had done very well before the Depression now found themselves working for her in the welfare department. Though others would treat the lawyers roughly, Doris treated them well.

Ahead of her time in many ways, Doris also traveled to Europe, where she loved Finland, but found Russia very depressing.

Little is known about Maud (b. 1896). She apparently went blind, and lived her life in South Dakota. Similarly, little is known about the only son, Billy (b. ~1901).

Figure 15. Ancestors Of David Hill Sr.

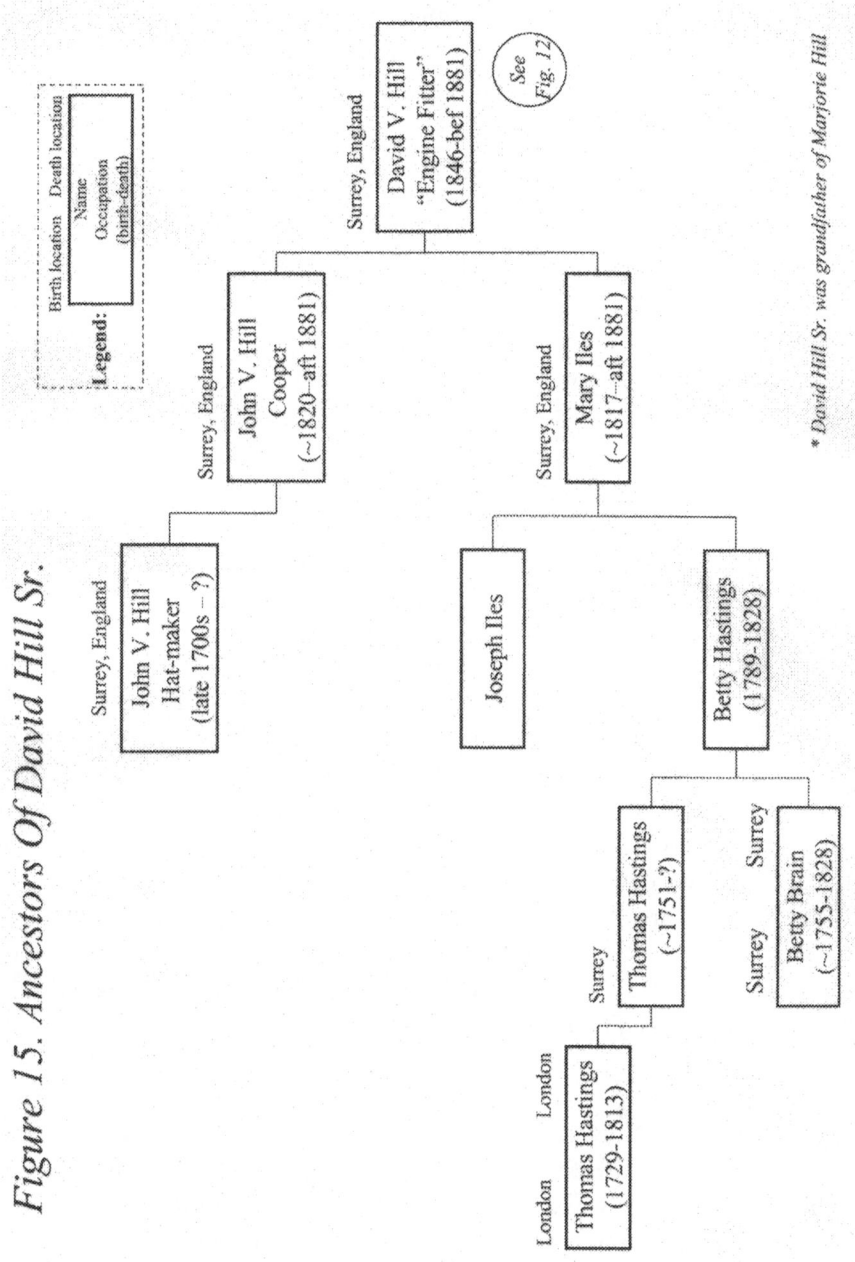

Legend:

Birth location · Death location
Name
Occupation
(birth–death)

Surrey, England
David V. Hill
"Engine Fitter"
(1846–bef 1881)

See Fig. 12

Surrey, England
John V. Hill
Cooper
(~1820–aft 1881)

Surrey, England
Mary Iles
(~1817–aft 1881)

Surrey, England
John V. Hill
Hat-maker
(late 1700s – ?)

Joseph Iles

Betty Hastings
(1789-1828)

Surrey
Thomas Hastings
(~1751-?)

Surrey · Surrey
Betty Brain
(~1755-1828)

London · London
Thomas Hastings
(1729-1813)

* *David Hill Sr. was grandfather of Marjorie Hill*

The father of David Hill was also named **David Hill**. Born in 1846, the elder David married **Mary Ross**. He indicated that his profession was "Engine Fitter." In the mid-1800s there were a number of "Engine Fitters" who worked on the London and South Western Railroad that connected London with Surrey and other Southern counties, so it's possible that the elder David was a mechanic for the railway. David died young, probably in the 1870s, and did not live to see his son get married in 1890.

The father of the elder David Hill was **John V. Hill**. Born around 1815 in Surrey, John was a cooper (i.e., barrel-maker), and in 1840 he married **Mary Ann Iles**. It is interesting to note that at least three generations of Hills (John, his son, and his grandson) all carried the middle name of Veasey, though it is not known why.

John V. Hill's father was another **John Hill**. He was probably born in the late 1700's, and listed his occupation as a hatter (hat-maker).

A family tree in the possession of David Ferguson, a grandson of David Hill, shows the ancestors of Mary Iles. Mary Iles parents were **Joseph Iles** and **Elizabeth "Betty" Hastings**. Joseph was a farrier, i.e., he shoed horses.

Betty Hastings parents were **Thomas Hastings** and **Betty Brain**. Thomas Hastings was in turn the son of another **Thomas Hastings** (1729–1813) who was born and buried in London.[117] It is suggested that this line eventually leads back to somehow associate with the Battle of Hastings in 1066, though no details or specific evidence are known.

My father has heard vague references to other genealogy work that was done on the Hill line, going much further back in time. People of note were a "Lord Percy,"…as well as a horse-thief. However, to date this other work has not been found, and no other details are known.

Hannah E. Campling's parents were **William H. Campling**, born around 1843 in Billangford, Norfolk County, England, and his wife **Hannah**, born around 1844 in Lowestoft, Suffolk County, England. Family lore is that Hannah, who served as a midwife, was loosely related to the Royal Family, but this has not been investigated or confirmed.[118] A photo of Hannah is included on the cover of this book (fourth row, fourth from left. Photo courtesy David Ferguson).

In the 1881 census, William listed his occupation as "plumber and glazier" and listed his home as Lowestoft, in Suffolk County, England. He was a painter and worked on restoration projects, including working on the ceiling of St. Paul's Cathedral in London.

In addition to Hannah, the Camplings had at least two other children, Eleanor and Kate Laura "Kitty." Kitty trained as a dressmaker and ran her own firm making dresses for some fairly grand clients. Professionally she was always known as "Madam Campling," though her married name was Mrs. Julius Prior. At one stage she employed twelve girls in her workshop.

William Campling is believed to have died in 1888, and his wife Hannah is thought to have died in 1919.[119]

Hannah's ancestry is in question. Based on census data, it certainly appears that her maiden name was Adams, and that her father was **James Adams**, born around 1800 in Pakefield, Suffolk County. James was a baker. However, other descendents suggest that her maiden name was Ramsey, and to date this question has not been completely resolved.[120]

APPENDIX

Family Members

Adams Campling, Hannah E. (1844–1919)

- Born 1844 in Lowestoft, Suffolk County, England. Died 2/17/1919[121]
- Wife of William Campling
- Mother of Hannah E. Campling (b. ~1870). Other children: Eleanor (7/20/1864–1950), and Kate Laura "Kitty" (12/12/1881–9/15/1969)
- Per 1881 British census: Age 33 (implies born ~1848?), born in Lowestoft, Suffolk, England

Adams, James (~1800–?)

- Father of Hannah E. Adams
- Died sometime after 1881
- Per 1881 British census:
  - Living with William Campling and Hannah Campling
  - Born ~1800 in Pakefield, Suffolk, England
  - Retired baker

Austin Jones, Deborah (1730–abt 1746)

- Born November 26, 1730 in Dighton MA
- Daughter of Jonah Austin and wife Priscilla
- Mother of Seth Jones
- Married Elijah Jones 24 Jan.1746/7 in Dighton MA

Austin, Jonah

- Lived in Dighton MA and Falmouth, Maine
- Father of Deborah Austin (b. 1730)

Austin, Jonah (1667–1755)

- Born August 17, 1667 in Taunton, MA
- Died about 1755 (will was probated March 22, 1755)
- Married Thomason Lincoln April 20, 1692 in Taunton, MA
- Father of Jonah Austin (b. 1695?)

Austin, Jonas[122]

- Baptized. February 28, 1629/30 in Tenterden, Kent, England
- Died May 10, 1676 in Taunton, MA
- Married Esther Reade May 8, 1641 (in Weymouth, MA?)
- Father of Jonah Austin (b. 1667)

Bartlett Thomas, Elizabeth (abt. 1810–1876)

- Born about 1810 in Weymouth, Cornwall, England (date of birth derived based on listed age of 41 on 1851 census)
- Married Anthony Thomas on November 8, 1829, in St. Gluvias
- Died January 19, 1876 (per Cornwall death records)

Brain, Betty (1750–1828)[123]

- Born 1750 in Camberwell, Surrey, England
- Died April 11, 1828 in Dulwich, Surrey, England

Campling Hill, Hannah "Annie" Elizabeth (1869–1938)

- Born August 28, 1869 in Lowestoft, Suffolk County, England
- At age 21, married David V. Hill 9/3/1890, in Lewisham, Kent County.
- Came to the U.S. in 1910[124]
- Daughter of William Campling and Hannah Adams

- Mother of Marjorie Hill (b. 1900); other children Maude, Mildred (b. July 1894, d. 1984), Doris (b. 11/10/1898, d. 12/12/1987), and William (b. 4/19/1906, d. 1987)[125]

- Died March 4, 1938 in New York City. Buried at Lake View Cemetery in Cleveland, Ohio (Sec 22 Lot 533-C).

Campling, William Hubbard (1843–1888)[126]

- Born ~1843 at Billingford, Norfolk, England

- Married Hannah E. Adams

- Occupation: Plumber and Glazier; also listed as decorator.

- Father of: Hannah E. Campling (b. 1870) and Kate Laura Campling (b ~1882).

- As of 1881 William resided at St. Peters Chapel 1 St. Peters Place; census place Lowestoft, Suffolk, England

- Believed to have died in 1888[127]

Edelen, Alexander (1843–aft 1880)

- Born April 20, 1843 in Maryland

- Married Georgianna Young February 28, 1867

- Farmer

- Father of Mary C. Edelen (b. 1872); other children Sarah (b. ~1867), John R. (b. ~1871), Margaret S. (b. ~1875), Francis E. (b. ~1878), George E. (b. ~1879)

Edelen Thomas, Mary Cornelia "Nealie" (1872–1963)[128]

- Born March 23, 1872 in Prince Georges County, Maryland[129]

- Wife of James C. Thomas

- Lived at 124 11th St. SE for over 50 years, until her death

  - In 1930 census, listed value of her home as $7000; also indicated she owned a radio

- Height was around 4'11"

- Mother of William R. Thomas (b. 1899). Other children: Helen (b. ~1902), James Jr. (~1904), Florence (~1910), Elizabeth (1916)

- As of 1920 census had 6 boarders living in her home; as of 1930 census her brother Guy and two boarders lived with her.

- Mary's siblings: Spencer, Charles, James, Robert, Frank, Hugh, Guy, Ella, Maggie, Ada

- Died 1963 at age 91 in Washington D.C.

Flowers Herdman, Nancy (~1825–186x?)

- Born ~1825 in Jackson County, current-day WV

- Date of death unclear—thought to be late 1860's

- Married Peter Herdman May 14, 1844 in Jackson County, WV (by Rev. Phillip Hall)

- Daughter of Mary Hall and Thomas Flowers

- Mother of 9, including James Herdman (b. 1845)

- Other children: Mary (1847), Thomas (1847), Hester (1851), Henry (1852), Ephriam (1854), Michael (1854), Rowena (1864), Jon (?)

Flowers, Thomas (~1781–~1845)

- Born ~1781 in PA

- Died ~1845

- Married Mary Hall

- Came to Jackson County about 1806[130]

- Father of Nancy Flowers

- One of the first settlers in Jackson County, early 1800's

Hall, Mary (1781–1858)

- Born ~1781 in PA

- Died 1858, Jackson County, WV at age 77

- Mother of Nancy Flowers

- Wife of Thomas Flowers

Hastings, Betty (1789–1828)[131]

- Born 1789, Died 1828

- Married Joseph Eyles September 2, 1809

- Mother of Mary Eyles; other children were Richard, Mary, Catherine, and Joseph

Hastings, Thomas (1729–1813)

- Born 1729 in Dulwich, London, England.

- Died May 30, 1813 in Dulwich, London, England

- Father of Thomas Hastings (b. ~1751)

Hastings, Thomas (~1751–?)

- Born ~1751 in Of, Dulwich, Surrey, England

- Married Betty Brain Nov 7, 1776 in St George Martyr, Southwark, London, England

- Father of Betty Hastings

Herdman, James Madison (1845–1927)[132]

- Born April 4, 1845 in Jackson County, current-day WV

- Son of Peter Herdman and Nancy Flowers

- Also known as "Polk" Herdman

- Married Perlina A. Jones December 31, 1872 in Mason County, WV

  - Marriage record indicated he was from Jackson County, she was from Mason County

- Father of four, including Nannie Herdman (b. 1876). Other children: Forest (b. 1874), Charles (b. 1875), (Annis—died in childbirth, 1879)

- Farmer

- Height 5'6"

- Joined United Brethren Church in 1880.

- Fought in Civil War for Confederacy, in Co. B, 22nd VA Infantry[133]

- Enlisted 9/22/1862 in Charleston
- Wounded in 1864
- Apparently fought in horrific battle of Cold Harbor
- Left Confederate army; declared oath to Union 2/22/1865 in Charleston and given amnesty
  - Couldn't read or write (per 1870 Jackson County census)
- Died October 14, 1927 in Buffalo, Putnam County, WV, at age 82
- Buried at Walker Chapel Church Cemetery, Putnam County, WV

Herdman Jones, Nancy "Nannie" (1876–1958)

- Born November 18, 1876, probably in Jackson County WV
- Died August 13, 1958 in Nitro, WV at age 81
- Buried at Creston Cemetery, WV
- Married Lorenzo D. Jones Feb 27, 1897, in Mason County, WV
  - Marriage record indicated both were from Mason County
- Mother of Opal Jones (b. 1900); Other children were Clive (b. 1898), Arol (b. 1899), and Hershel (b. ~1904)
- Also raised 3 Sayre kids: Dwight, Gordon, and Dorn
- Lived on farm in Mason County

Herdman, Peter (1822–1907)

- Born December 22, 1822 in Pennsylvania
- Married first wife Nancy Flowers May 14, 1844 in Jackson County WV[134]
  - Peter and Nancy had 10 children, including James Herdman (b. 1845)
  - Other children: Mary (1847), Thomas (1847), Hester (1851), Henry (1852), Ephriam (1854), Michael (1854), L.J (1858), Elijah (1861), Rowena (1864)
- Married second wife Martha McDade November 22, 1874[135] (he was 52, she was 17)

- Martha had been born ~1858 in Virginia

- Per 1850 census:

  - Gave name as "Peter Hardman"—age 26, born PA

  - "May Flowers" also lived in the home—age 69—Nancy's grand-mother??

  - Did not own land

- Per 1870 Jackson County census: Owned $350 in real estate, $250 in personal property

- Per 1880 census

  - Peter age 57, farmer, himself and both parents born in PA

  - Wife Martha age 22

- Military service[136]

  - Was a Private in 141st Militia (also known as Jackson County Home Guards), a local Union militia responsible for maintaining order, and fighting various Confederate guerillas. Served in "B" Company of Capt. J. M. Burditt. Enrolled July 20, 1863, in Jackson County (one month after WV gained statehood 6/20/1863)

  - At time of Civil War he apparently listed his home as Cow Run, Jackson County

- Owned land:

  - Purchased land (50 acres) in 1869 from his Captain in 141st Regiment. Value of Peter's land in 1870 stated as $350.

  - Also purchased land from David Sayre in 1866?

- Died May 24, 1907 at Cow Run in Putnam County, WV at age 84

- Buried at Cherry Grove Cemetery, Jackson County, WV (name on tombstone spelled as "Hurdman")

Hill, David Veasey "Sr." (1846–bef. 1890)

- Born December 4, 1846. Son of John Veasey Hill and Mary Ann Iles Hill.

- Family address at the time was 3 Verdant (?) Place, Hen and Chicken Lane, St. Peter Walworth subdistrict, St. Mary Newington district, Surrey County.

- Married Mary Ross (probably between 1865 and 1870)

- Occupation listed as "Engine Fitter."

- Father of David V. Hill (b. 1870)

- Died relatively young. Not found in 1881 census; listed as deceased on marriage record of his son in 1890.

Hill, David Veasey "Jr." (1870–1930)

- Born January 31, 1870 Camberwell district, Surrey County (outside London). Son of David Veasey Hill and Mary Ross. Family address was 3 Alfred Street, St. George's Road, Camberwell.

- At age 20 married Hannah E. Campling September 3, 1890 at St. Augustine (?) Parish Church, Lewisham, Kent. Gave his occupation as clerk. Indicated his father was deceased. Ceremony was witnessed by Eleanor Sophie Campling and Joseph James Hill.

- As of 1891 census of England:

  - Home: 27 Whitfield (??) Road, Administrative County of London; Civil parish: Lewisham; Ecclesiastical parish: St. Mary

  - David and Hannah shared a home with James J Adams & his wife Mary, and with William Hill. William is 2 years younger, likely his brother?

- As of 1900, lived at 35 Arabin Road, Brockley, London (per birth certificate of Marjorie Hill)

  - Occupation was "Commercial Troweller"

- Came to U.S. in 1908, settled in Pierre, South Dakota in 1908

- Per declaration of intention for citizenship filed 2/24/1911:

  - Occupation: Fireman and engineer

  - 5'10" 175 pounds

  - Came to the U.S. on the St. Paul of America Line from Southampton, England, arriving New York around August 28, 1908

- As of 1915 state census, lived in Pierre, South Dakota

- Lived in Cleveland from 1918 to 1930. Last known address was 2066 E. 77th Street.

- Member of Episcopal church

- Father of five children including Marjorie Hill (b. 1900); other children Maude, Mildred (b. July 1894, d. 1984), Doris (b. 11/10/1898 d. 12/12/1987), and William (b. 4/19/1906, d. 1987)[137]

- Died 4/27/30 in Cleveland, Ohio. Buried at Lake View Cemetery in Cleveland 4/29/30 (grave location is Section 22, Lot 533).

Hill, John Veasey ("Jr.") (abt 1815–aft 1880)

- Born ~1815 at Southward (?) Surrey County, England

- Father of David V. Hill "Sr." (born 1846).

- Married Mary Ann Iles August 23, 1840. Per the marriage certificate:

  - They were married at St. Peter's Church Walworth, in the parish of St. Mary Newington, Surrey County

  - John lived at 10 King's Row

  - One of the witnesses was Henry Veasey Hill, though it is not known how Henry was related to John.

- Occupation was given as Cooper (barrel-maker).

- As of 1881 census, John and Mary lived at 27 Standard Street, Newington, Surrey County.

Hill, John Veasey ("Sr.") (late 1700's–?)

- Father of John Veasey Hill (b. abt 1815). Based on having a son in 1815, it is assumed that John "Sr." was born in the late 1700s.

- Only known information about him is from his son John's marriage record

Hill Thomas, Marjorie (Margueret) Kate (1900–1964)

- Born January 5, 1900 in London, England (Lewisham district). Daughter of David Veasey Hill and Hannah Campling Hill

- Came to the U.S. in 1910, settled in South Dakota[138]

- Mother of Don Thomas (b. 1928), other child was Jean Thomas Draper (b. 1932)

- Died October 14, 1963 in West Virginia; buried at Cunningham Memorial Park, St. Albans, WV.

Iles, Joseph[139]

- Perhaps born ~1790–1800

- Married Betty Hastings (perhaps also known as Elizabeth or Betsy) on September 2, 1809

- Father of Mary Iles; other children were Richard, Mary, Betty, Catherine, and Joseph

- Per his daughter's marriage record, Joseph's occupation was farrier (hatmaker)

Iles Hill, Mary Ann

- Perhaps born ~1810–1820

- Mother of David Hill "Sr." (b. 1846)

- Married John V. Hill August 23, 1840. Per the marriage certificate:

  - They were married at St. Peter's Church Walworth, in the parish of St. Mary Newington, Surrey County

  - Mary lived at Herne (?) Hill, in Camberwell

Jones, Charles A (~1826–?)

- Born VA ~1826 (Age 24 in 1850 Mason County census)

- Married to Jane Minturn October 19, 1849 in Mason County (per Mason County Marriage records)

- Father of Perlina A. Jones (b. 1849); other children: Maria (b. ~1829), Delila (b. ~1831), Isaac (b. ~1834), Ann (b. ~1838), Valencourt (b. ~1840)

- Lived in Mason County (Perlina said she lived there when married in 1873)

Jones, Cornelius Sr.[140]

- Born in Portsmouth, RI?
- Married Mercy Corey ~1661 in Portsmouth, RI
- May have been father of Cornelius Jones (b. ~1693), but not confirmed. Other child was Ichabod Jones.

Jones, Cornelius Jr. (1693?–abt 1745)[141]

- Perhaps born late 1600's (perhaps 11/1/1693 in Essex County, MA?)
- Died Berkley MA ~1745
- Married wife Abigail ~1718
- Known to have lived in Taunton MA as of ~1722; whereabouts prior to that are unknown
- Occupation: "shipwright"
- Father of Elijah Jones (b. 4/11/1725); other children were Priscilla (b. 8/16/1719, died before May 1741), Henry (b. 4/25/1721), Cornelius (b. 3/21/1723), Jara (b. 12/17/1728), Charles (b. 12/14/1730), Abigail (b. 2/3/1732), Benjamin (b. 4/20/1736), Sylvester (b. 9/6/1738), Priscilla (b. 5/8/1741), Bethany (b. 1744 or 1745)

Jones, Elijah (1725–abt 1770?)[142]

- Born April 11, 1725, in Dighton, Bristol County, Massachusetts
- Son of Cornelius Jones and Abagail
- Married Deborah Austin April 9, 1747 In Berkley, Bristol County, Massachusetts
- Served as Private in Foot Company of Taunton 1757
- Occupation: Shipwright and caulker
- Father of 8 children including Seth Jones (b. 1755)
- Other children: Elijah (b. 1747), Priscilla (b. 1749), Aquilla (b. 1751), Increase (1752–1825?), Income (b. 1757), Benson (b. abt. 1760)
- Perhaps died around 1770

Jones, John Paul (1848–1929)

- Born March 16, 1848, Meigs County, Ohio
- Son of Silas Jones and Dorothy Roush
- Married Caroline Sayre Feb 3, 1870, in Jackson County, WV[143]
- Father of Lorenzo Jones (b. 1873)
- Children included Sarah (b. 1879), Earnest Valentine (b. 1875), David Wallace (b. 1871), Lettie (b. 1881), Minnie (b. 1885), Silas Vernon (b. 1887), Dorothy (?) (b. 1889), Arla (b. abt 1894)
- Farmer in Mason County as of 1880 census
- Died June 13, 1929 in Mason County, WV at age 80[144]
- Buried at Creston Cemetery, Mason County WV

Jones, Lorenzo Dow (1873–1905)

- Born 1873 in Ohio[145] (assumed in Meigs County)
- Married Nancy (Nannie) J. Herdman Feb 27, 1897, in Mason County, WV[146]
- Father of Opal Jones (b. 1901)
- Other children: Clive (b. 2/9/1898), Arol (b. 10/21/1899), and Hershel
- Lived in Mason County as of 1900 census
- Died 1905 of either "consumption" (tuberculosis) or pneumonia, at age 32
- Buried at Creston Cemetery, Mason County WV

Jones Martin, Opal Lena (1901–1981)

- Born 10/28/01 in Mason County WV[147]
- Died February 21, 1981 at age 79, in Kanawha County
- Daughter of Lorenzo D. Jones and Nannie Herdman
- Married Thad Martin (assumed in late 1920's)
- Mother of Reba Martin (b. 1930)
- Other children: Tom (b. 1937), Eddie, Edrie

Jones Herdman, Perlina Angeline (1849–1879)

- Born ~1849 (gave age as 23 when married in 1872)

  - Age listed as 10 months in 1850 Mason County census

- Daughter of Charles Jones and Jane Minturn

- Married James Herdman 12/31/1872 in Mason County WV

- Mother of four, including Nannie Herdman (b. 1876)

- Other children: Forest (b. 1874), Charles (b. 1875), (Annis—died in childbirth, 1879)

- Died during childbirth 1879[148]

Jones, Seth (1755–1824)[149]

- Born September 28, 1755 in Dighton Massachusetts (raised in Bristol County?)

- Son of Elijah Jones

- Veteran of Revolutionary War, did three tours of duty:

  - Enlisted spring 1775 in Capt. Peter Pitts Company, Col. Timothy Walkers Massachusetts regiment. Private; served 8 months; fought in Battle of Bunker Hill.

  - Served one month Aug/Sept 1777 in Capt John Petty's Company, Col. Williams Vermont Regiment; fought at Battle of Bennington.

  - March 1778 enlisted in Capt. James Rosecrans Company, 5th New York Regiment, served until January 1782. Was at Battle of White Plains.

- Apparently grew-up in Dighton MA; Moved to Putney VT after Revolutionary War; then moved from Putney VT to Ohio around 1797–1799

- Father of 18 children by two wives, including Silas Jones (by Esther Adams).

- Married Sarah Pitts September 27, 1778 in Dighton, Massachusetts.

  - Sarah was sister of Seth's Captain Peter Pitts from the War

- Children: Sarah (b. 1780), Seth (b. 1782), Betsy (b. 1784), Serena (b. 1786), Phillip (b. 1788), Henry (b. 1790), Hannah (b. 1792), Patty (b. 1794), Sally (b. 1798), Charles (b. 1800)

- Married Esther Adams August 26, 1810 in Meigs County, Ohio.

  - Children: Lewis (b. 1813), Hetta (b. 1815), Lawnor (b. 1817), Milton (b. 1820)

- Died September 10, 1824 in Graham Station (now Racine), Meigs County, Ohio, at age 69

- Buried at Letart Falls Cemetery, Meigs County, Ohio

Jones, Silas (1811–1901)

- Born June 9, 1811, in Letart Falls, Meigs County, Ohio

- "Farmed out" to a cabinet-maker as a young boy, may not have known his own family?

- James Hall appointed as guardian for 13-year old Silas after his fathers death

- Farmer who owned $1000 of real estate as of 1850 Ohio census, which grew to $7000 by 1870 census

- Married Dorothy Roush August 9, 1833 in Meigs County, OH[150]

- Father of 7 children, including John Paul Jones (b. 1848)[151]

- Other children: Mary (b. 1837), Stores (b. 1839), Esther (b. 1842), Alice (b. 1844), Lewis (b. 1846), John (b. 1848)

- Sources: 1850 Ohio census

- Died July 23, 1901 in Racine, Meigs County, Ohio at age 90

- Buried Greenwood Cemetery, Meigs County, Ohio

Little, Sarah (1761–1846)

- Born 1761

- Died 1846 (in Letart Falls, Meigs County, Ohio or in Evans, Jackson County, WV)

- Mother of Daniel Sayre (b. 1785)

- Other children: Anna Belle (b. 1787), Ezekiel (b. 1789), Joel (b. 1791), Rachel (b. 1791), Sarah (b. ~1795), Hannah (b. ~1796), Abel (b. 1799)

Martin, Benjamin Franklin (1869–1948)

- Born July 19, 1869 in Kanawha County, WV

- Son of William Martin and Rachel Persinger

- Married Laura Ann Wilkinson March 5, 1899

- Had 7 children, including Thad Martin (b. 1904).

- Other children: Roy (b. 1900), Noble (b. 1906), Pearl (b. 1901), Sylvia Gladys (b. 1912), Mildred Pauline (b. 1920)

- Died May 10, 1948 in Putnam County, WV at age 78[152]

- Buried at Ortin Heights cemetery, Nitro WV

Martin Thomas, Reba Alice (1930–)

- Born April 16, 1930

- Daughter of Thad Martin and Opal Jones

- Mother of Robert Thomas (b. 1960) and Susan Thomas Wulf (b. 1955)

- Lives today in Chattanooga, TN

Martin, Thad (1903–1976)

- Born September 17, 1903[153]

- Son of Benjamin Martin and Laura Wilkinson

- Worked as an "Oiler" maintaining machines at Viscose (manufacturer of rayon) in Nitro for ~5 years ~WWII[154]

- Father of Reba Martin (b. 1930)

- Died April 2, 1976 in Kanawha County; buried at Cunningham Cemetery, St. Albans WV

Martin, William B. (~1839–1916)

- Born ~1839 in (Kanawha County?) then-Virginia

- Married Rachel Persinger[155]:

- Married May 2, 1866 in Kanawha County
- William was 26, bride Rachel Persinger was 18
- Her father was present (no mention of his father)
- Minister was Joshua Jenkins (or Thomas Harmon?)
- Father of 11 children, including Benjamin Martin (b. 1869)
- Other children[156]: Elizabeth (1865–1940), William (1866–1910), James (1868–1937), Silas (1871–1942), Josephine (b. 1876), Levi (1877–1963), Lucinda (1879–1920), Cora Bell (1880–1957), Juda Emaline (1882–1964), Victoria (1887–1915)
- Per 1870 Kanawha County census:
  - Taken at Union Township, Sissonville Post Office
  - William was a farmer, and could both read and write
  - Did not own real estate; value of personal property listed as $100
  - Wife Rachael could not read or write
- Per 1880 census:
  - Didn't provide a middle initial
  - Age 41 implies born ~1839
  - He was born in WV; Father born in OH, mother born in WV
  - Wife Rachel age 37, father born WV, mother born VA
- Died 1916 at age ~76. Buried at Clark Cemetery, Putnam County WV (10 miles west of Sissonville).

Minturn, James C (~1800–?)[157]

- Born ~1800 in NY (age 50 in 1850 census)
- Father of Jane Minturn
- Farmer in Mason County as of 1850 census
- Wife Mary Ann (Edwards?) (b. ~1803)
- Other children: Maria (b. ~1829), Delila (b. ~1831), Isaac (b. ~1834), Ann (b. ~1838), Valencourt (b. ~1840)

Minturn Jones, Jane (~1824–?)

- Born ~1824

  - Gave age as 26 in 1850 Mason County census

- Mother of Perlina Angeline Jones (per Becky Hinton's family notes and 1850 census)

- Married Charles Jones October 19, 1849 in Mason County

- Daughter of James Minturn and wife Mary

- Note that surname spelled "Mintum" on marriage recording, but father seems to give name as "Minturn"

Persinger, Charles (~1841–?)

- Possibly born ~1841, son of Kenneth Persinger??

- May be father of Virginia Persinger (b. 1862), but not confirmed

- Husband of Emma Hall

Persinger, Kenneth (~1803–1890)

- Born ~1803 in Kanawha County VA

- Died July 6, 1890 in Putnam County[158]

- Married Lucinda Reynolds (on April 7, 1831?)

- Son of Jacob Persinger and Ursula Blake

- Father of Rachel Persinger (b. ~1848)[159]

  - Other children: Margaret (b. ~1831), Ursula (b. ~1833), Mary (b. ~1836), Sarah (b. ~1840), Charles (b. ~1841), Anderson (b. ~1844)

- Per 1850 Kanawha County census

  - Kenneth age 46, farmer born in VA

- Per 1870 census:

  - Was on preceding page of William Martin and Rachel (Persinger) Martin

  - Kenneth a farmer, age 67 (implies born ~1803), born in "VA now WV")

Persinger Martin, Rachel (~1848–1918)

- Born ~1848 in Kanawha County[160]
- Married William Martin[161]:
  - Marriage date: May 2, 1866
  - William was 26, bride Rachel Persinger was 18
  - Her father was present (no mention of his father)
  - Minister was Joshua Jenkins
- Born in WV, father from WV, mother from VA
- Note that on Benjamin's death certificate his mother's name is listed as "Rachel Hill," but other records prove this incorrect. Likely reflects that Benjamin's children simply didn't know their mothers maiden name.
- Died 1918, buried at Clark Cemetery, Putnam County, WV

Persinger Wilkinson, Virginia Ann (1862–1897)

- Born March 10, 1862
- May have been daughter of Charles Persinger and Emma Hill
- Married David A. Wilkinson, maybe around 1876?
- Mother of ten, including Larra (Laura) Wilkinson
- Other children: Bessie (1886), Minnie May (1878), Dora (1880), Ida (1883), James (1884), Mary (1888), Martha (1889), Ola (1891), Nancy (1895)
- Died 1897 at age 35, perhaps during childbirth.[162]

Rausch, Johann Adam (1711–1786)[163]

- Original "Roush" to settle in America
- Born 1711
- Came from Darstadt, Germany, around 1735; settled in Shenandoah County, VA
- Died 1786, buried in Shenandoah County, VA
- Married Susannah Schler around 1740, in America

- All children except one Anglicized name to "Roush"

Reynolds Persinger, Lucinda (~1807–?)

- Wife of Kenneth Persinger (married 1831?)
- Mother of Rachel Persinger (b. ~1848)[164]
  - Other children: Margaret (b. ~1831), Ursula (b. ~1833), Mary (b. ~1836), Sarah (b. ~1840), Charles (b. ~1841), Anderson (b. ~1844)
- Per 1850 Kanawha County census
  - Wife Lucinda age 42, born VA
- Per 1870 census:
  - Was on preceding page of William Martin and Rachel (Persinger) Martin
  - Wife Lucinda age 63 (implies born ~1807), born in VA

Ross Hill, Mary[165]

- Probably born in 1840's
- Assumed to have lived in London
- Wife of Charles Hill
- Mother of David Hill (b. 1870)

Roush Jones, Dorothy (1817–?)

- Born April 17, 1817 in Ohio[166]
- Married Silas Jones August 9, 1833, in Meigs County OH
- Father of 7 children, including John Paul Jones (b. 1848)
- Other children: Mary (b. 1837), Stores (b. 1839), Esther (b. 1842), Alice (b. 1844), Lewis (b. 1846), Silas (b. 1849)

Roush, Henry Sr.

- Born 1752 in Shenandoah County, VA
- Died 1831, buried in Plants Cemetery in Meigs County, Ohio
- Father of Henry Roush (b. 1782)

- Served in John Tipton's Company in Revolutionary War

Roush, Henry (1782–1865)

- Born November 24, 1782
- Died June 14, 1865 at Letart, Ohio
- Married Anna Belle Sayre January 16, 1802
- Father of Dorothy Roush (b. 1817)

Sayre Roush, Anna Belle (1787–1892) [167]

- Born June 4, 1787 in Morgantown, PA (now WV)
- Died April 3 (or January 31?) 1892 at age 104
- Married Henry Roush January 16, 1802
- Mother of Dorothy Roush
- Lived to see her great-great-great-granddaughter
- Note: Anna Belle is #1328 in Banta

Sayre Jones, Caroline (1848–1909)

- Born Feb 1848 in current-day West Virginia
- Lived in Jackson County when got married to John Paul Jones
- Died 1909, assumed in Mason County, WV
- Buried at Creston Cemetery
- Married John Paul Jones February 3, 1870
- Mother of Lorenzo Jones (b. 1873)

Sayre, Daniel (~1624–1708) [168]

- Probably born in Bedfordshire, England about 1624
- Died 1708 in New York
- Married Hannah Foster ~1666 in Suffolk County, NY
- Occupation: Whaler and farmer
- Son of Thomas Sayre

- Father of Samuel Sayre
- Note: Daniel is #3 in Banta

Sayre, Daniel (?-1760)[169]

- Died 1760
- Married Rebecca Bond
- Blacksmith in Elizabeth NJ
- Thought to be son of Samuel Sayre
- Father of David Sayre (b. 1736)
- Note: Daniel is #63 in Banta

Sayre, Daniel (1785–1866)[170]

- Father of David Sayre (b. 1810)
- Died March 7, 1866
- Farmer and local preacher of Methodist Church in Mason County, WV
- Note: Daniel is #1329 in Banta

Sayre, David (1736–1826)[171]

- Born Essex County NJ May 30, 1736
- Died July 11, 1826 at Letart Falls, Ohio
- Lived in "northwest VA" towards close of 18th century, and purchased "large tracts of land"
- Married Hannah Frazier in 1758
- Blacksmith
- Note: David is #199 in Banta

Sayre, David (1762–?)[172]

- Born December 18, 1762
- Married Sarah Little
- Father of Daniel Sayre (b. 1785)

- Received warrant 1799 for 300 acres in Monongalia County, VA (Revolutionary War bounty??)
- Built grist mill at Letart Falls, Meigs County, OH in 1810
- Note: David is #549 in Banta

Sayre, David (1810–1895)[173]

- Born October 20, 1810, probably in current-day Jackson County, WV
- Died February 15, 1895, and buried in the David Sayre family cemetery at Cow Run, Jackson County WV
- Son of Daniel Sayre and Sarah Hall
- Farmer in Angerona, WV; owned >1500 acres in Mason County
- 11 Children from 4 marriages, including Caroline Sayre (by Minerva Stone)
- Married first wife Minerva Stone September 27, 1838
  - Other Children: George (b. 1839), Lucy (b. 1842), Daniel (b. 1845), and Reuben (b. 1850)
- Other wives and children:
  - Married Marthenia Hill 8/28/1851; children Lucian (b. 1853), Oscar (b. 1856), Minerva (b. 1859), David (b. 1864), Ira (b. 1867)
  - Married Mary Stephenson July 18, 1872
  - Married Nancy Scantling July 27, 1876
- Owned $5000 in real estate as of 1860 census
- Note: David is #2702 in Banta

Sayre, Samuel (~1668–~1707)[174]

- Father of Daniel Sayre
- Lived in Elizabeth, NJ
- Note: Samuel is #20 in Banta

Sayre, Thomas (~1597–1670)[175]

- Born ~1597 in Leighton, Bedfordshire, England

- Baptized July 7, 1597
- Died 1670 in Southampton (Long Island, NY) at age 73
- Son of Francis Sayre and Elizabeth Atkins
- Father of Daniel Sayre (b. ~1620); line eventually leads to David Sayre (b. 1810)
- First in (our) Sayre line to come to America
- Farmer and tanner

Stone Sayre, Minerva (1819–1851)[176]

- Born March 25, 1819 in Greene County, PA
- Stone family came to what is now Jackson County in 1823
- Died April 13, 1851 (perhaps during childbirth??)
- Married David Sayre on September 27, 1838
- Daughter of George Stone and Lucinda Miller. Per their 1850 census form for Jackson County, George was a farmer, born in Pennsylvania around 1792.
- Mother of 5 children, including Caroline Sayre (b. 1848)
- Other children: George (b. 1839), Lucy Ann (b. 1842), Daniel (b. 1845), Reuben (b. 1850)

Symons Thomas, Jane (1839–1914)

- Born in St. Noet, Cornwall, England (per 1881 census)
  - Father's name was Samuel Symons
  - Birth date most likely 1839 as implied on her marriage certificate, though in later census listings she would provide inconsistent dates for her age and data of birth
    - Gave age as 38 in 1881 UK census (implies birth date 1843)
    - Gave age as 66 in 1910 U.S. census (implies birth date 1844)
    - In 1900 U.S. census gives birth date as Feb. 1846
- At age 26 married James Cornish Thomas ("Sr") on 4/29/1865 in Bodmin district of Cornwall County.

- At this time both he and his wife listed their town of residence as Hamett St. Neot
- Emigrated to U.S. in 1884
- Gave birth to 13 children, including James C. Thomas (b. 1867). Other children: May (b. 1866), Emma (b. 1869), John (b. 1870), Samuel (b. 1873), Richard (b. 1875), Elizabeth (b. 1877), Emilie (b. 1879)

  - Five of the children died relatively young.

- In England, name was spelled "Symons," but in the U.S. was sometimes spelled "Simmons"
- Died at age 70 on February 19, 1914, and buried at Congressional Cemetery in Washington D.C. Last residence had been Cherrydale, Virginia.[177]

Thomas, Anthony Plummer (1805–1884)

- Baptized April 7, 1805 in St. Gluvias, Cornwall, England. Son of James and Katherine Thomas.
- At age 25 he married Elizabeth Bartlett on November 8, 1829, in St. Gluvias.
- Father of James Thomas (born 1833); other children included John (b. ~1830), Catherine (b. ~1836), Charles William? (b. ~1842), Samuel (b. ~1843), Anthony (b. ~1846), Elizabeth (b. ~1848), Richard (b. ~1850), Amelia (b. ~1852), Harriet (b. ~1856)
- As of 1881 he was a retired farmer widower living with his daughter Amelia and two boarders, at 3 Central Cottage, in Falmouth, Cornwall County, England
- Died 9/28/1884 at his residence (Central Cottage, Castle Hill), Falmouth, Cornwall County, England

Thomas, Donald Charles (1928–)

- Born September 19, 1928 in Cleveland, Ohio
- Father of Robert Thomas (b. 1960) and Susan Thomas (b. 1955)
- Married Reba Martin April 30, 1954
- Graduated Virginia Tech 1950

- Chemical Engineer
- Retired Col. Army Chemical Corps
- Lives today in Chattanooga, TN

Thomas, James (1768—?)

- Baptized January 25, 1768. Son of John and Catherine Thomas.
- At age 26 married Katherine Paule October 22, 1794, in Redruth (10 miles from Falmouth, Cornwall).

  - James made his "mark" on the marriage record, indicating that he could not write.

- Father of Anthony Thomas (b. 1805)

Thomas, James Cornish "Sr." (1833–1902)

- Born May 1833 at Budock, Cornwall County, England. Son of Anthony Plummer Thomas and his wife Elizabeth. Baptized 10/6/1833.
- At age 31 married Jane Symons (Simmons) on 4/29/1865 in Bodmin district of Cornwall County. At this time both he and his wife listed their town of residence as Hamett St. Neot.
- Was a farmer while in England
- In the 1860s the family lived in Mylor (based on birth locations of children as specified in 1881 census)
- As of 1871 census the family lived at Trenowah Farm in St. Austell, Ecclesiastical District of Charlestown, Cornwall County, and farmed 58 acres with the help of 2 employees.
- Brought family to U.S. 1884 on the *Italy*, arriving New York May 7, 1884.
- Per 1881 British Census:

  - Age 43 (implies born 1838; probably a typo and was actually written "1833")
  - Farmer with 45 acres
  - Birthplace: Falmouth, Cornwall, England

- Dwelling on Charlestown Road; Census Place was St. Austell, Cornwall, England

- Father of James Thomas (b. 1867). Other children: Mary "May" (1865–1937?), Emma Jane (b. 1866), Emma Jane (1868–1896), John R. (1869–1956), William Henry "Willie" (b. 1871), Samuel (b. 1872), Richard (1875–1920), Elizabeth "Bess" (1876–1948), Emilia (b. 1878), Harry (b. 1882)

  - Apparently the first child named Emma Jane died very young, and the next girl was given the same name.

  - Willie apparently died before 1881, as his name was not included either the 1881 census, or on the passenger list with the rest of the family when they came to the U.S.

- Gave occupation as Gardener while in the U.S.

- Per 1890 D.C. City Directory: Lived with James Jr. at 612 I Street Southeast

- Per 1900 U.S. census:

  - James C. born May 1833 in England; occupation is gardener

  - Jane born Feb. 1846; had 13 children, 8 living

  - Renting a home (at 104 11th St. NE?)

- Died June 6, 1902. Last residence had been 104 11th Street SE, Washington D.C.[178] Buried at Congressional Cemetery, Washington, D.C. Grave location: Range 20, site 66.

Thomas, James Cornish "Jr." (1867–1918)

- Born September 7, 1867 in sub-district of Mylor, district of Falmouth, Cornwall County, England (per birth certificate)

  - Note that other birthdates, all incorrect, appear for James Jr.

    - He stated "9/7/1862" in records for USS Albatross, but it's possible that this represents him fibbing his age in order to get into the service.

    - More confusing is that date of 9/7/1862 appears in an entry from a family bible. Entry in Bible appears wrong given chronological listing.

- His 1900 census indicates November 1867, but it's possible that information was supplied by somebody else at the household in error.

- Emigrated to U.S. with his family in 1884

- Enrolled in U.S. Navy for one year 7/11/1884, was fireman on "The Albatross."

- Height 5'5", weight 135 pounds

- Address in 1891: 612 I Street Southeast (lived with James Sr.), per 1890 Washington D.C. City Directory

- At age 30 married Mary Edelen August 3, 1898 in Washington D.C.

- Listed occupation as "steam engineer"—was engineer who ran Washington Monument (elevator?)

- As of 1900 census lived at the home of his brother Samuel at 249 (?) 12th Street SE

- As of 1910 census lived at 124 11th St. SE

- Father of William R (b. 1899); other children: Helen (b. ~1902), James Jr. (~1904), Florence (~1910), Elizabeth (1916)

- Died March 14, 1918 in Washington D.C.) at age of 50. Last known address was 124 11th St. SE, Washington D.C.[179]

Thomas Draper, Jean (1932–)

- Born February 1932

- Daughter of WR Thomas and Marjorie Hill; sister of Don Thomas

- Married Chuck Draper

- Lives today in Springfield, Illinois

Thomas, John (abt 1740–?)

- Father of James Thomas (b. 1768). Assuming he was in his twenties when married, then he was perhaps born in the 1740s.

Thomas, Robert William (1960–)

- Born March 8, 1960 in Charleston, WV

- Son of Donald Thomas and Reba Martin
- Graduated UC Santa Barbara 1983
- Married Michelle Hernandez March 14, 1992
- Electrical Engineer
- Lives today in Palo Alto, CA

Thomas Wulf, Susan Lynn (1955–)

- Born November 22, 1955
- Daughter of Donald Thomas and Reba Martin
- Graduated from the University of Tennessee at Chattanooga in 1999
- Teacher
- Married Jim Wulf 12/31/76
- Mother of Matthew Robert Wulf (b. 1978)
- Lives today in Chattanooga TN

Thomas, William Robert "Tommy" (1899–1975)

- Born December 30, 1899 in Washington D.C.
- Lived with parents in Washington D.C. as of 1920 census; occupation was draftsman at Maryland State Archives[180]
- Perhaps took some classes at George Washington University (per his obituary)
- Married Marjorie Kathryn Hill April 27, 1927, in Cleveland
- Father of Don Thomas (b. 1928) and Jean Thomas Draper (b. 1932), both by first wife Marjorie Kate Hill
- In 1930 census, Tommy indicated that he was renting a house in Baltimore for $90 per month, and that he had a radio.
- After death of Marjorie in 1963 Tommy later married Jackie Vandyne
- Died June 16, 1975 in Cape Coral, Florida. Buried at Memorial Gardens Cemetery, Ft. Myers, Florida.

Vandyne Thomas, Judith K "Jackie" (1913–1997)

- Born September 3, 1913. Father was Otis Vandine (~1887–7/15/63) and mother was Maggie Vandine (~1883–2/11/53)

- Second wife of WR Thomas

- Died January 3, 1997 in Chattanooga, TN. Buried at Memorial Gardens Cemetery, Ft. Myers, Florida.

Wilkinson, David (1798–1857)

- Born 1798 in Virginia

- Died (September 18?) 1857 at age 59

- Married Nancy Thomas

- Father of 7 children, including David Wilkinson (b. 1835)

- Farmer in Kanawha County (current-WV) as of 1850 census

- Other children: Zibe (b. 1842), James (b. 1832), Ambrose (b. 1822), Joseph (b. 1827), William (b. 1829), Ransome (b. 1838)

Wilkinson, David Almagro (1835–1918)

- Born March 27, 1835 in current-day West Virginia

- Father of 15 children, including Laura Wilkinson (b. 1881), by two wives

- Married Ann Older January 18, 1855 (Ann born in England Dec 26, 1837[181])

  - Children: John E. (b. 3/101856), Jeannette (b. 5/1/1858), Andrew B. (b. 11/25/1860), Joannah (b. 10/5/1864)

- Married second wife Virginia Persinger May 10, 1877 in Kanawha County

  - Children: Minnie Mae (b. 4/18/1878), Dora Bell (b. 4/6/1880), Larra (Laura) Ann (b. 9/19/1881), Ida W. (b. 5/10/1883), James E. (b. 11/30/1884), Bessie E. (b. 8/7/1886), Mary E (b. 3/5/1888), Martha Odessa (b. 11/18/1889), Ose Ola (b. 5/23/1891), Nancy S. (8/10/1894)

- Lived in Kanawha County as of 1880 census

- Died November 2, 1918 (or 10/2/18?) at age 83

Wilkinson Martin, Larra (Laura) (1881–1960)

- Born September (6th or 19th,) 1881, probably in Kanawha County, WV
- Daughter of David Wilkinson and Virginia Persinger
- Married Benjamin Martin on March 5, 1899
- Had 7 children, including Thad Martin (b. 1904).
- Other children: Roy (b. 1900), Noble (b. 1906), Pearl (b. 1901), Sylvia Gladys (b. 1912), Mildred Pauline (b. 1920)
- Died December 9, 1960 in Nitro, WV at age 79[182]
- Buried at Ortin Heights cemetery, Nitro WV

Wulf, James Robert (1954–)

- Born March 11, 1954
- Husband of Susan Thomas
- Graduate of Marshall University, Huntington WV
- Teacher and coach
- Lives today in Chattanooga TN

Wulf, Matthew Robert (1978–)

- Born January 6, 1978
- Son of Susan Thomas and Jim Wulf
- Lives today in Chattanooga TN

Bibliography

Publications

1. William Wallace Austin, Jr., William Allen Day and Edith Austin Moore, *Jonah Austin 1598–1683 of Taunton, Massachusetts Sailed on Hercules of Sandwich in March 1634/5,* 1975

2. Banta, Theodore, *Sayre Family: Lineage of Thomas Sayre, a founder of Southampton,* The De Vinne Press, New York, 1901

3. Cohen, Stan, *The Civil War in West Virginia, A Pictorial History,* Gateway Printing, 1976

4. Hite, Delmer R., *Roster of Jackson County Civil War Soldiers,* 1972

5. House, John A, *Pioneers of Jackson County, West Virginia. History of Mill Creek and Sandy Valley and Its Early Settlement.* 1906. Published by WebRoots, Inc., 2001, Betty Briggs

6. Larkin, Stillman Carter, *The Pioneer History of Meigs County,* Meigs County Historical Society c1982

7. Lowry, Terry *"22nd Virginia Infantry,"* H.E. Howard Inc., 1988

8. McTeer, Frances Davis, Julia Bumpus Berndt and Frederick C Warner. *Several Jones Families in Bristol Co, Massachusetts,* 1977

9. Mitchell, Joseph B. *Decisive Battles of the American Revolution.* Mockingbird Books, 1962.

10. Sayre, Ralph Hall. *Sayre Family: Another 100 Years,* Volume I, iUniverse Inc., 2003

11. Swango, Maxine Virginia May and Richard F. Legg, *Early Kanawha County Marriages, 1855–1867,* Kanawha Valley Genealogical Society, South Charleston WV, 1981–89

12. Jackson County Historical Society, Inc., Jackson County WV. *Jackson County Past and Present, 1990*, Walsworth Publishing, 1997

13. *Jackson County 141st Militia*, Knightstep Imprints, 1995

14. Mason County History Book Committee and Don Mills, *History of Mason County, WV 1987*

15. Roush, Lester LeRoy, *History Of The Roush Family In America*, Shenandoah Publishing House, Strasburg, VA, 1928

16. Donnelly, Mary Louise, *Major William Boarman, Charles County, Maryland (1630–1709)—His Descendants and Allied Families*, 1990

17. Newman, Harry Wright, *Charles County Gentry*, Genealogical Publishing Company, Inc., Baltimore, 1971.

18. Gardiner, Thomas R., *Gardiner Generations and Relations*, Vol I.

Other Sources:

19. Letters and records of West Virginia State Archives, Jackson County 141st Militia Collection

20. Richmond National Battlefield website, http://www.nps.gov/rich/ri_cold.htm

21. http://www.usahistory.info/Revolutionary-War/Bunker-Hill.html, Converted from Henry William Elson's *History of the United States of America* The MacMillan Company, New York, 1904

22. The American Revolution.org: www.theamericanrevolution.org/battles/bat_ben.asp

23. Roush family website: www.roush.org

24. For background on U.S. Presidents: www. whitehouse.gov/history/presidents

25. West Virginia archives: www.wvculture.org/history/statehoo.html

26. Taunton MA Vital Records to 1850 (marriages). Published by New England Genealogical Society, Boston MA. www.rays-place.com/town/ma/taunton/marage-a.htm

27. Taunton, MA Vital Records to 1850, Births, Surnames Starting with A. Published by New England Genealogical Society, Boston MA. www.rays-place.com/town/ma/taunton/birth-a.htm

28. Gatrell, Jay Dean, *Localized Innovation, A Geography Of The Petrochemical Industry in the Kanawha Valley, WV*, 1999 (dissertation posted at http://etd.wvu.edu//ETDS/E752/ch6_7.pdf)

29. McCoy, Ron, *Men Who Matched the Mountains*, http://www.real-mccoys.com/feud.html

About the Author

Bob Thomas, son of Don and Reba Thomas, was born in 1960 in St. Albans, West Virginia. He lived there until the family moved to California when he was fourteen years old. Bob still has a strong affinity for West Virginia.

Bob makes his living in the computer industry of Silicon Valley, and whenever possible enjoys traveling and writing. He lives today with his wife Michelle in Palo Alto, California.

Endnotes

1. Per Don and Reba Thomas, and per a dissertation by Jay Dean Gatrell, *Localized Innovation, A Geography Of The Petrochemical Industry in the Kanawha Valley, WV,* posted on the West Virginia University website at http://etd.wvu.edu/ETDS/E752/ch6_7.pdf.

2. Minnie Herdman was probably an aunt of Nannie Herdman.

3. David Hart indicates that all of the children of John Paul Jones attended Lone Cedar School.

4. Per Becky Hinton, daughter of Earnest Jones, who was a son of Hershel Jones, who was son of Nannie Jones.

5. Dick Hart, a distant relative, indicated that he had always understood the cause of Lorenzo's death to be from pneumonia after rolling logs in the winter.

6. "Nancy J Herdman," age 3, is listed in the Russell household in the 1880 census, Union district, Jackson County, West Virginia.

7. Per Becky Hinton.

8. Copy of tax assessment is in possession of Reba Martin Thomas.

9. Per Becky Hinton.

10. Per interview of Earnest Jones, August 2003, Charleston, WV. Earnest was the son of Hershel Jones, who in turn was one of four children of Lorenzo and Nannie.

11. Per Tom Martin, July 2003.

12. Date of death per Benjamin Martin's death certificate.

13. Benjamin and Laura are buried together at Ortin cemetery in Nitro. On the tombstone is given their wedding date of March 5, 1899.

14. Dates of birth and death for Laura Wilkinson originally sourced from her death certificate; also verified from other sources.

15. Roy is buried at Ortin cemetery in Nitro, and his grave marker gives his date of death as August 2, 1958.

16. Per Dick Hart.

17. Story of John Paul Jones' workhorse Ben is from David Hart.

18. Becky Hinton indicated that John Paul donated the land for Creston Cemetery. Based on research done by his mother Veta, David Hart indicated that John Paul remarried after Caroline's death, and that the name of his second wife was Jane. This is also substantiated by a photo in the possession of Janis Tennant, which has cryptic references to "grandma Jane" and John Paul Jones. Jane's maiden name is not known for sure, though it's possible that she was a Minturn.

19. Per Becky Hinton

20. Per *Several Jones Families in Bristol, MA*, page 33.

21. Information regarding Seth Jones is from his Revolutionary War Pension file, provided by the U.S. National Archives and Records Administration, Washington D.C. Materials in the Pension file also validate that Silas Jones was the son of Seth.

22. There is some question as to whether the New York service was by "our" Seth Jones. Documents in Seth's Pension file raise this question, but do not make any firm conclusion.

23. Per service records of Seth Jones.

24. Per Sandi Lee Craig, a distant Jones relative

25. As cited by James Williams in the service records of Seth Jones.

26. Per *Pioneer History of Meigs County, Ohio, to 1949*, by Edgar Ervin.

27. From *Central Ohio Genealogical Notes* published in the *National Genealogical Society Quarterly*, Vol. 26, as cited in *Several Jones Families in Bristol County, MA*.

28. *Several Jones Families in Bristol County, MA*, page 33.

29. Information on Elijah and Cornelius Jones sourced from *Several Jones Families in Bristol County, MA* This document also verifies that Seth was the son of Elijah, and that Silas was son of Seth.

30. Comments on potential parents of Cornelius Jones from an undocumented source on the web, so accuracy has not been validated.

31. *Dictionary of Surnames*, Patrick Hanks and Favia Hodges, Oxford University Press, New York, 1988

32. Per *Sayre Family*, Theodore Banta, 1901.

33. Per article referenced in Banta, 1901.

34. Documents supplied by the Roush family indicate that Henry Roush served in the Revolutionary War, but he is apparently not listed in the pension files index (*Genealogical Abstracts of Revolutionary War Pension Files*, abstracted by Virgil White, National Historical Publishing Company, Waynesboro TN, 1992.

35. Per Roush descendent Keith Ashley.

36. Information on distant Roush ancestors is per *History Of The Roush Family in America*, by Lester Leroy Roush; and comments from Keith Ashley, a Roush descendent.

37. "Passage to America, 1750," EyeWitness to History, www.eyewitnesstohistory.com (2000), includes excerpts from the diary of Gottlieb Mittelberger, a German who came to Philadelphia in 1750, and provides graphic description of these difficulties.

38. Information on David Sayre and his ancestors is sourced from two outstanding family histories done on the Sayre line: *Sayre Family*, Theodore Banta, 1901; and *Sayre Family, Another 100 Years*, by Ralph Sayre, 2003, iUniverse Publishing.

39. Per *History of Mason County*, 1987, contributed article by Charlotte Sayre.

40. Posted on ancestry.com; also included in *Sayre Family* by Banta, 1901.

41. James Herdman birth date obtained from his death certificate, and also verified in other records.

42. *22nd Virginia Infantry*, by Terry Lowry.

43. James Herdman's service records, provided by the U.S. National Archives, give his date of enlistment, unit, and mention his injury.

44. Most of the information about the 22nd Virginia was sourced from *22nd Virginia Infantry* by Terry Lowry. James Herdman's service records were obtained from the United States Archives.

45. Richmond National Battlefield: Cold Harbor. Website http://www.nps.gov/rich/ri_cold.htm

46. Reference to James Minturn's service in the Civil War was written on the back of a family photograph.

47. In the 1880 U.S. census, and others, Peter indicated that both his father and mother were born in Pennsylvania.

48. Records of the 141st available at the West Virginia Archives include service records of Peter Herdman. Note that Peter is also sometimes referenced as "Hardman." He could not read or write, so it's likely that he simply spoke his name to others who wrote it, and thus the potential for different spellings of the name.

49. Per *Jackson County 141st Militia*, Knightstep Imprints, Ripley WV, March 1995, and also per review of records of 141st available at West Virginia archives.

50. 1870 census shows James living in Peter's house.

51. The photograph of Peter and James Herdman was probably taken by a traveling photographer. Traveling photographers covered many rural areas in the second half of the 19th century.

52. Per Mason County marriage records.

53. Per hand-written obituary of James Herdman, a copy of which is in possession of Reba Thomas. This same note also states that James volunteered for the Civil War on 9/22/1862.

54. 1880 U.S. census for Peter Herdman family, Cologne, Mason County, West Virginia.

55. Census records indicate that Phillip Herdman lived in Fayette County PA in 1830, and then Jackson County (then-Virginia) in 1840. Then a Phillip Herdman shows up in Wood County, which borders Jackson County, in the 1850 census. Names of children and wives were only given in census listings as of 1850, so additional research is required in order to verify whether Phillip is indeed father of Peter. This 1850 census indicated that Philip was born in Virginia, but that the two children then living with him were born in Pennsylvania, consistent with Peter Herdman having been born in PA.

56. Per *Pioneers of Jackson County*, by John House, and *Jackson County Past and Present, 1990*.

57. Per *Abstracts of Revolutionary War Pension Files*: Thomas Flowers S22773, New Jersey Line, born Salem Cunty N 8/19/1761, moved to Philadelphia in 1795. However, no relationship between this man and the father of Nancy Flowers has been confirmed.

58. This is derived from the 1850 Mason County census listings, which show "Perlina A," age 10 months, living with father Charles A Jones and his wife Jane. That family lived next door to "James C. Minturn, age 50, and it is assumed that James gave land to his daughter Jane and her husband Charles Jones. Mason County marriage records spell Jane's name as "Mintum," but it is assumed that this was an error in transcribing from the handwritten records.

59. Per Becky Hinton.

60. West Virginia separated from Virginia and gained statehood in 1863. Kanawha County was originally formed in 1788.

61. The 1870 census for Marion Township, Kanawha County, shows William Martin with wife Rachel and 1-year old son Benjamin.

62. Per *Early Kanawha County Marriages 1855–1867*.

63. In census forms of the times, respondents were typically asked to provide the state of birth for themselves, as well as for their mother and father. In each of his census forms, William indicated his father was from Ohio.

64. Crystal Clark, a common descendant of "our" William Martin, indicates that she has a photo of William Martin with his sister Leanna, and that the Baptist Preacher William Martin indeed had children William and "Lenna" listed in the 1850 census. In this 1850 census listing, young William is listed as 14 years old, whereas "our" William was born in 1839. Ages in census listings were often in error, so this may not be significant. Of further question is that "our" William had indicated in census listings that his father was born in Ohio, and the Baptist Preacher William Martin indicated that he had been born in Virginia.

65. Per David Wilkinson's family records.

66. Per 1870 census, David Wilkinson, Union township, Kanawha County, West Virginia owned $500 of land and had an additional $100 estate

67. The father of Ann Older was perhaps "Eward" (Edward?) B. Older, who was 55 years old in the 1860 Kanawha County census, and who indicated

he had been born in England. His wife Mary was also 55, and had also been born in England.

68. Per Laura Wilkinson Martin's death certificate.

69. Notes from a family bible kept by David Wilkinson indicate that a child was born March 26, 1897, but did not survive. It is speculated that Virginia Persinger died during the birth of this child.

70. Per 1850 census of Kanawha County, then part of Virginia.

71. 1880 census for Putnam County lists Charles Persinger and wife Emily of Pocatalico, Putnam County, WV, which is consistent with where Virginia is thought to have lived.

72. Per 1880 census, Kanawha County.

73. Per family records cited by Mrs. Terri L. Wiseman Smith; also seems to be indicated by Kenneth living next door to Jacob, who was some 20 years older, in the 1850 census.

74. Information on distant Persinger ancestry is from various sources presented in an online Persinger family forum on Yahoo Groups.

75. From *The Life Of Jacob Persinger*, by Joseph Persinger, Strugeon, Mo., 1861, and an article in the Roanoke Times by Marty Horne.

76. Per WR Thomas birth certificate.

77. William is included in a McKinley Tech yearbook that is in the possession of Don Thomas. It appears that McKinley was a military school.

78. The stories of the encounter with President Taft, and of seeing Walter Johnson pitch, are memories Bob has from talking with his grandfather in the 1960's.

79. Tommy indicated on his 1920 census that he worked at the Maryland Archives.

80. Per Tommy's sister Elizabeth.

81. Per 1920 census, the family lived on Keswick (?) Road, and shared a rental house with three other people. Tommy was working as a mechanical engineer, and paying rent of $90 per month.

82. Information regarding moves to New York and Asheville are per Don's sister Jean Thomas Draper.

83. Per Jean Thomas Draper. Also note that Taft was President from 1909 to 1913.

84. Per 1920 census.

85. A wedding invitation in the Thomas family specifies a wedding date of April 27, 1927.

86. Per Jean Thomas Draper.

87. Information on parents of Jackie Vandyne is from obituaries of her parents, in possession of Don Thomas.

88. Information regarding service on *Albatross* is per discharge papers in family possession.

89. http://www.multied.com/Navy/Steamer/Albatross.html

90. *Revisiting the 1918 Flu*, transcript of interview with Elizabeth Farnsworth, http://www.pbs.org/newshour/bb/health/march97/1918_3-24.html, and http://www.pbs.org/wgbh/amex/influenza/timeline/. Also see http://www.haverford.edu/biology/edwards/disease/viral_essays/redicanvirus.htm

91. James Thomas and Mary Edelen were married August 3, 1898. The ceremony was officiated by an Arthur S. Johnson, and the marriage record indicates an "office station" of Keeton, Washington Parish, D.C. Arthur Johnson also officiated at the marriages of both Florence and Elizabeth Thomas in 1935 and 1945, respectively, according to Elizabeth.

92. Mary Edelen's 1900 census indicates that she was born in March 1872 in Maryland.

93. Information on Nealie Edelen is from an interview with Elizabeth Goodnight in August, 2003.

94. Purchase date confirmed by original deed. Mary died May 14, 1963, per daily records of Washington's Old Congressional Cemetery.

95. Per Tommy's sister Elizabeth

96. Tidbits on the siblings of James Thomas were from Elizabeth Goodnight, and from notes made on an old family photograph.

97. Per Cornwall Family History Society, http://www.cornwallfhs.com/, and www.cornwall-calling.co.uk/folklore-and-legend/shorthi.htm

98. Per passenger list of the "Italy," 1884, ancestry.com.

99. See *Ship Travel In Third Class*, http://www.cruisemates.com/articles/ onboard/steerage.cfm. Data on passenger count of the *Italy* is from the ship's passenger list.

100. Per records daily logs from Washington's Old Congressional Cemetery, James Sr. died on June 6, 1902, and Jane died February 19, 1914.

101. James was baptized January 25, 1768, so he was likely born a few weeks earlier.

102. Per "Index of Marriage Licenses, Prince George's County Maryland, 1777–1886," by Helen Brown, Genealogical Publication Company, Baltimore, 1973, pages 72 and 248.

103. Per "Major William Boarman, Charles County, Maryland (1630–1709)—His Descendants and Allied Families," by Mary Louise Donnelly, 1990, pages 29, 46, 47, 73, 74.

104. *Information on Prince George's County is largely from "A COUNTY WITH RICH HISTORY: PRINCE GEORGE'S COUNTY HISTORY, by Alan Virta, at* http://www.pghistory.org/PG/PG300/history.html.

105. Excellent information on the Edelen line is provided at http://www. ghgcorp.com/edelen/People1.html

106. Marriage certificate indicates David Hill and Hannah Campling were married September 3, 1890. Note that David apparently called his wife "Annie," as that's the name entered for her on their 1920 census form.

107. Interestingly, David Hill's name does not show up in the immigration records of Ellis Island.

108. "Auxiliary Cruisers St. Paul and St. Louis," by Patrick McSherry, http:// www.spanamwar.com/stpaul.htm, and http://www.fortunecity. com/littleitaly/amalfi/13/shipqs.htm

109. Per 1915 South Dakota census.

110. Per David Ferguson

111. Per David Ferguson, a grandson of David Hill. David Ferguson is also the source for the information that David Hill was in the scrap iron business in England.

112. Per 1920 Ohio census and death certificate of David Hill.

113. Burial location of David Hill is from his death certificate. Information regarding burial of Garfield and Rockefeller is from www.lakeview cemetery.org.

114. Per Campling family records provided by David Vale.

115. FDR story, and all the information regarding Marjorie Hill's siblings, was provided by David Ferguson.

116. Per burial records from Lake View Cemetery.

117. Note that descendants of David Hill were provided from a family tree, which apparently had been thoroughly researched in England. The dates of birth and death for each have been derived from other sources.

118. Per David Vale

119. Date of death for Hannah is per Campling family records provided by David Vale. William Campling was referenced on his daughter's 1890 marriage certificate, so he died sometime after 1890.

120. David Vale, another descendent of Hannah Campling, indicates that many years ago his ancestors specifically said that the maiden name of Hannah Campling's mother was Ramsey.

121. Supplied by David Vale, per family records

122. Per *English Origins of New England Families*, a reprint of articles that appeared in the New England Historical and Genealogical Register, Genealogical Publishing Co, Baltimore, 1984, Vol 1, pages 248–253.

123. Names of ancestors of David Hill were obtained from a family tree in possession of David Ferguson.

124. Per 1915 census filing in South Dakota.

125. Per family records of David Vale

126. Information on William Campling is from marriage record of Hannah Campling and David Hill, and per 1881 British census.

127. Per David Vale family records

128. Information on Nealie Edelen is primarily from daughter Elizabeth Goodnight and grandchildren Don and Jean Thomas.

129. Per St. Paul's Parish Records, Baden in Prince Georges County, MD

130. Per *Pioneers of Jackson County* by John House.

131. Information on Hastings line is per Hill family tree in possession of David Ferguson.

132. Per marriage record and death certificate of James Herdman. Information of Perlina and Annis dying in childbirth is from a hand-written obituary of James, a copy of which is in possession of Reba Thomas.

133. Per James "Polk" Herdman service records, National Archives and Records Administration.

134. Per *Jackson County Marriages 1831–1879*.

135. Per marriage certificate, courtesy Joann Herdman.

136. Per *Jackson County 141st Militia*, Knightstep Publishing, Ripley WV 1995.

137. Per family records of David Vale

138. Per 1915 South Dakota census.

139. Information on Joseph and Mary Eyles from family tree in possession of David Ferguson.

140. Information on Cornelius Jones Sr. obtained from posting on ancestry.com, but has not been confirmed.

141. *Several Jones Families in Bristol County, MA*.

142. Ibid.

143. Per WV Register of Marriages, Jackson County Courthouse, Ripley WV.

144. Per John Paul Jones death certificate.

145. 1880 census for John Paul Jones indicates 7-year old son Lorenzo was born in Ohio.

146. Per *Mason County Marriages, 1886–1900*.

147. Per General Index and Register of Births, Mason County WV.

148. Per handwritten obituary of James Herdman, copy in possession of Reba Martin Thomas.

149. Information on Seth Jones was obtained from his Revolutionary War Pension file, U.S. National Archives and Records Administration.

150. Per *Meigs County, Ohio, Marriages, 1819–1913*.

151. 1850 Meigs County census for Silas Jones shows 2-year old son John Paul. Same census form indicates that Esther Koontz, widow of Silas' father Seth, lived next door. It is speculated that Esther gave Silas some of the Bounty Land from Seth's Revolutionary War service, but this has not been confirmed.

152. Per Benjamin Martin death certificate.

153. Per daughter Reba Martin Thomas.

154. Per Tom Martin.

155. Per *Early Kanawha County Marriages 1855–1867*.

156. Primarily from 1880 census. Dates of death are from Crystal Clark, a Martin descendent, who has posted her understanding of the Martin family tree at rootsweb.com.

157. Per 1850 census.

158. Per family records of Mrs. Terri L. Wiseman Smith.

159. Per 1850 census.

160. Per 1850 census, where she was listed as Kenneth Persinger's 2-year old daughter.

161. Per *Early Kanawha County Marriages 1855–1867*.

162. Information recorded by David Wilkinson shows that an un-named baby Wilkinson was born March 26, 1897. Coupled with Virginia Persinger's death date of 1897, it is possible that mother and child both died during childbirth.

163. Information on Roush men is primarily from http://www.roush.org/ninebro.htm; and Keith Ashley, a Roush descendent.

164. Per 1850 census

165. Per Hill family tree in possession of David Ferguson.

166. Per *Sayre Family*, Banta.

167. Ibid.

168. Per *Sayre, Another 100 Years* by Ralph Sayre, and *Sayre Family*, by Banta.

169. Source: Banta, *Sayre Family*.

170. Ibid.

171. ibid.

172. ibid.

173. *Sayre Family, Another 100 Years*, by Ralph Sayre.

174. Source: Banta, *Sayre Family*.

175. From *Sayre Family*, by Banta; and "*Sayre Family, Another 100 Years*" by Ralph Sayre.

176. From *Sayre Family, Another 100 Years* by Ralph Sayre.

177. Per records supplied by Congressional Cemetery, Washington D.C.

178. Per records supplied by Congressional Cemetery, Washington D.C.

179. ibid

180. Per 1920 census.

181. Birthdates for Wilkinson children are as recorded in David Wilkinson's family bible. A copy of this sheet was provided by Penny Cottrill.

182. Per Laura Wilkinson death certificate.

Index

0-595-33412-1